Chinese Cooking
AT • THE • ACADEMY

JAY HARLOW
Writer

JILL FOX
Editor

KEVIN SANCHEZ
Photographer

SUSAN MASSEY-WEIL
Food Stylist

LIZ ROSS
Photographic Stylist

CALIFORNIA CULINARY ACADEMY

Jay Harlow, a free-lance writer and cooking teacher, is author of several cookbooks and a weekly column in the *San Francisco Chronicle*. His other books for the California Culinary Academy cookbook series include *Enjoying American Wines, Southeast Asian Cooking,* and the Pacific States chapter of *Regional American Classics*. A former restaurant chef, he has also served on the board of directors of the San Francisco Professional Food Society and as the first Administrative Director of The American Institute of Wine and Food.

The California Culinary Academy In the forefront of American institutions leading the culinary renaissance in this country, the California Culinary Academy in San Francisco has gained a reputation as one of the most outstanding professional chef training schools in the world. With a teaching staff recruited from the best restaurants of Western Europe, the Academy educates students from around the world in the preparation of classical cuisine. The recipes in this book were created in consultation with the chefs of the Academy. For information about the Academy, write the Office of the Dean, California Culinary Academy, 625 Polk Street, San Francisco, CA 94102.

Front Cover

This Chinese New Year's banquet of braised duck (page 33), accompanied by stir-fried vegetables and steamed rice (page 103), showcases the basic cooking techniques associated with Chinese cooking: simmering, braising, steaming (see page 63); roasting, grilling, smoking (page 85); stir-frying and deep-frying (page 39).

Title Page

Fillet of Ocean Dragon, a dramatic transformation of fried flounder, presents easily served, boneless fillets on a "platter" of the fish frame, with head and tail intact (page 52).

Back Cover

Upper: Eight-Treasure Chicken (page 82) is a show stopper dish. A boned chicken is stuffed with rice and sausage and then steamed inside bamboo leaves. Although this cooking technique takes some practice, the results are obviously spectacular. Moist-heat cooking techniques begin on page 63.

Lower: Barbecued Beef, Beijing Style (page 96), is a variation on Mongolian barbecue. An assortment of dipping sauces and condiments adds to the excitement of this Beijing specialty.

Special Thanks to

Victoria Bunting, Ceramic Showcase, Joyce Jue, Mary Francis Porter, Elaine Ratner, Sloan Miyasato, Susan Tselos, Susan White, and Martin Yan.

Contributors

Additional Photographers
Victor Budnik, front cover
Clyde Childress, page 37
Alan Copeland, at Academy
Marshall Gordon, techniques
Kit Morris, author and chefs, at left

Additional Food Stylist
Doug Warne, techniques

Calligraphers
Keith Carlson, Chuck Wertman

Copy Chief
Melinda E. Levine

Editorial Coordinator
Kate Rider

Copyeditor
Rebecca Pepper

Indexer
Elinor Lindheimer

Proofreader
Leslie Tilley

Layout editor
Linda M. Bouchard

Composition
Bob Miller/Octavo

Series Format Design
Linda Hinrichs, Carol Kramer

Cover Design
Nina Bookbinder

Lithographed in the USA.

The California Culinary Academy Series is published by the staff of The Cole Group.

Publisher
Brete C. Harrison

Associate Publisher
James Connolly

Director of Operations
Linda Hauck

Director of Production
Steve Lux

Production Assistant
Dotti Hydue

Copyright © 1987, 1993 The Cole Group
All rights reserved under international and Pan-American copyright conventions.

A B C D E F G H
3 4 5 6 7 8 9 0

ISBN 1-56426-037-2
CIP 92-30276

Address all inquiries to
The Cole Group
4415 Sonoma Highway/ PO Box 4089
Santa Rosa, CA 95402-4089
(707) 538-0492 FAX (707) 538-0497

Distributed to the book trade by
Publishers Group West

C O N T E N T S

Chinese Cooking Techniques

The same cooking techniques and fundamental ingredients form the basic fabric of Chinese cuisine in all its regional variations.

The Chinese Kitchen

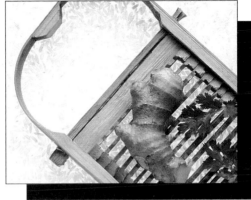

Chinese cooking includes such regional variations as the familiar Cantonese style of the south, the highly seasoned foods of Sichuan and Hunan, and the Mandarin cuisine of the imperial court, to name just a few. All these regional cuisines are based on a fairly small number of basic cooking techniques. Some, like stir-frying, are uniquely Chinese inventions; others, such as stewing and roasting, are cosmopolitan methods that the Chinese have refined to their own style. In this book, you will learn the fundamental techniques of Chinese cooking through recipes from all regions of China, grouped by cooking technique.

THE TASTES OF CHINA

Chinese cuisine, with all its regional diversity, is the product of thousands of years of development and refinement. Through the milennia, as the Chinese have traded with, conquered, or been conquered by neighboring peoples, they have absorbed foreign cultural influences while remaining distinctively Chinese. In the same way, as the cuisine adapted to local food resources and introduced ingredients, Chinese food habits, cooking techniques, and attitudes toward food have stayed basically the same.

It is important to remember that the term "Chinese food" is as broad a generalization as "European food." China covers an immense area, from the tropics to as far north as the Aleutian Islands, and from the fertile lowlands of the Yellow and Yangtze rivers to the Himalayas and the high, arid plains of Central Asia.

With a population of nearly a billion people, China is as diverse ethnically as it is geographically. Besides the Han Chinese, the dominant ethnic group, there are dozens of ethnic minorities, each with its own cultural traditions and language. Even among the Han, there are many regional dialects, which can be as different from one another as Spanish is from Portuguese and Italian.

Of course, the variety of climates means there is a wide range of foods grown in China. The residents of the semiarid, barley- and wheat-growing northwest can hardly be expected to have the same diet as those of the moist, subtropical southeast.

Still, for all this diversity, all Chinese have certain cultural traits in common, many of them connected to food. Although the foods vary, the regional cuisines of China are united by two main elements: the composition of meals (relatively little meat, more emphasis on vegetables and especially grain) and a basic set of cooking techniques refined over thousands of years.

Fan and Tsai

If there is such a thing as a typical Chinese meal, it consists of a generous portion of rice or other grain food, a smaller quantity of vegetables, and a still smaller amount of meat, poultry, or seafood. The Chinese have traditionally divided food into two categories: *fan*, which covers all grain foods, and *tsai*, which loosely translates as "dishes" and covers nearly everything else. Fan is by far the more important of the two, nutritionally, economically, and symbolically. Depending on the food resources of the region, it may be rice, wheat in the form of bread or noodles, or a variety of other grains, including corn, millet, barley, and sorghum. These cereal foods provide most of the calories and essential nutrients in the Chinese diet. Like the phrase "our daily bread," fan symbolizes all food.

This is not to imply that tsai is not important in the Chinese scheme of things. In fact, most of the techniques in this book have to do with preparing tsai. These foods provide essential nutrients to complement those in grains. And, of course, they offer a much wider range of flavors and textures to make the meal more appetizing.

Yin and Yang

One of the central concepts of Chinese philosophy, science, and art is the harmony of opposite qualities—*yin* and *yang*. Yin is identified with cool, moist, yielding things and the feminine principle; yang, with all that is warm, dry, firm, "masculine."

The system of yin and yang applies to food as well and is an important part of traditional Chinese medicine. In the Chinese view, a proper balance of yin and yang is essential to good health, and disease represents an imbalance. Restoring balance is largely a matter of eating the right food—that is, one with the proper yin or yang qualities.

Both foods and cooking methods are classified as yin or yang depending on whether they provide a warming or cooling effect on the body.

Fish, and especially shellfish, are considered yin or "cold" foods; green vegetables and most beans are also yin, but less so. Grains are essentially neutral, neither yin nor yang. Oily foods and red meats are more yang than yin, and hot seasonings such as ginger, garlic, and pepper are extremely yang. Thus, ginger is almost always served with fish, and meat is paired with plenty of fresh vegetables.

Cooking methods also affect the balance of yin and yang. Roasting, stir-frying, and frying in oil increase the yang in foods, whereas gentle simmering or steaming is more yin. Serving foods cold also makes them more yin.

Don't think, however, that you have to become an expert on the yin-yang classifications of foods to cook delicious Chinese meals. There is really nothing mysterious about the principle; just remember the basic ideas of balance and contrast. Besides juxtaposing different flavors, such as sweet and salty, include contrasting colors, textures, and intensities of flavor. In Cashew Velvet Chicken (see page 41), for example, crunchy vegetables and nuts are combined with tender cubes of chicken in a silky sauce. Tiny bits of minced ginger offer both another texture and little nuggets of intense flavor.

Yin and yang do not always have to be balanced within the same dish, but there should be a balance within the meal. Thus, a deep-fried dish (very yang) should be accompanied by other dishes cooked by yin methods such as steaming or simmering.

A perfect Chinese meal balances opposite qualities, as symbolized by yang and yin—strong and mild flavors, firm and soft textures, dry and moist dishes.

Chinese cooks carefully balance five basic flavors, represented here by some common ingredients; clockwise from lower left, they are sweet, bitter, salty, sour, and hot. Not all of these flavors are found in every dish, but a good meal should include all in harmony.

The Five Flavors

In addition to the properties of yin and yang, the Chinese recognize five fundamental flavors: sweet, sour, hot, bitter, and salty. These too must be kept in balance in a properly designed Chinese meal, if not necessarily in a single dish.

Sweet foods in Chinese cuisine include not only sugar, honey, and the various sweet-tasting fruits and vegetables, but also the sweetish flavor of some kinds of shellfish. Even water from certain sources, particularly springs and mountain streams, is described as sweet.

Sour ingredients include vinegars (made chiefly from rice or other grains), citrus fruits in the south, and various pickled vegetables.

Hot chiles and peppercorns are relatively late arrivals in China, although they are now firmly established flavors. Ginger is the most common hot flavor, and the one with the longest history.

Bitterness is a flavor more appreciated in China than in much of the West. Even among the Chinese, however, a little bitterness goes a long way. With the notable exception of bitter melon (see page 31), few foods are simply bitter; most combine a touch of bitterness with a sweeter flavor, as in turnips, cabbages, and certain other vegetables.

Salt is used in Chinese cooking in many forms other than mere table salt. Condiments and preserved foods such as soy sauce, various soybean pastes, fermented black beans, pickled vegetables, and ham often provide all the salt a dish needs. But salt crystals are also used, especially where the dark color of soy sauce would be inappropriate. The experienced cook takes all the salty ingredients in a dish into account in the overall balance of flavors.

The Chinese Diet and Health

Whether you subscribe to Chinese medical theory or not, there is no question that the Chinese diet is more healthful than that of the industrialized West. For the last decade or so, more and more Western nutritionists have been advocating a diet lower in meats, fats, and refined carbohydrates and higher in complex carbohydrates (vegetables and starches) than is contained in the typical North American diet. What these modern scientists describe is what the Chinese have been eating for thousands of years. Because Chinese cooking relies so heavily on grains and fresh vegetables, it naturally provides plenty of complex carbohydrates. Lightly cooking vegetables preserves more of their nutritional value than boiling them endlessly. Meat has always been used rather sparingly in authentic Chinese cooking, originally because of availablity and economic reasons but now as a matter of taste and habit.

But it is especially in the use of fat that we can learn from Chinese cooks. Some fat is necessary in the diet to help the body metabolize certain vitamins, but the typical Western diet is excessively fatty. Chinese cooking uses fats for flavor and texture. True, many dishes are cooked with oil, and bad restaurant cooking is often excessively oily. The Chinese use less meat, and meat is typically trimmed of its excess fat before it is cooked, so even a stir-fried dish can be quite low in fat. Lean fish, pork, and poultry are far more common than beef in most areas (well-trimmed pork is actually leaner than similarly trimmed beef, as the meat is not marbled with fat). Butterfat is virtually unknown in the Chinese diet, except among certain minorities. All in all, the Chinese diet contains a healthier proportion of fat than most of us are accustomed to.

To those concerned with the amount of salt in their diets, Chinese food may seem quite salty. Soy sauce and other condiments contain plenty of salt, but they are generally used in small quantities. Rice, which makes up a large proportion of a typical Chinese meal, is always cooked without salt. Taken as a whole, a Chinese meal need not contain any more salt than a Western meal. Of course, the amounts of any salty ingredient can be varied according to taste. For those who need to reduce their salt intake, there are now reduced-sodium soy sauces on the market.

Special Feature

WHAT TO DRINK WITH CHINESE FOOD

Although tea is the universal beverage of China (see Tea Time, Chinese Style, page 118), other beverages are sometimes served. Soup actually serves as a beverage in some meals, with tea following at the end.

Chiu, usually translated as "wine," is the Chinese term that covers all alcoholic beverages. Most are made from rice or other grains, and they vary in strength from Shaoxing and similar rice wines (about 15 to 20 percent alcohol, the same as sherry) to clear, 100-proof distilled spirits similar to vodka. Shaoxing is typically served warm, in small glasses or cups much like Japanese sake cups. Its rich, sherrylike flavor goes well with a variety of Chinese foods. The high-proof varieties of *chiu* may also be served with meals, especially formal banquets, where tiny glasses are tossed down as toasts between courses.

Beer is relatively new in China, a legacy of the German occupation of Shandong province around the turn of the century. China's principal beer, the excellent European-style Tsingtao lager, is made in the German-built brewery in the city of the same name (Qingdao in the new spelling). Beer goes especially well with the chile-laced dishes of the southwest and the garlic-and-green onion flavors of the north, but many diners find it the ideal beverage with all sorts of Chinese and Western foods.

Wine and Chinese cuisine are not natural partners, unlike the wines and foods of southern Europe. Grapes are not native to China and are only grown in a few limited areas; only a tiny bit of grape wine is produced. Still, the diversity of both Chinese cuisine and Western wines provides plenty of chances for exciting combinations.

White wines are most often recommended with Chinese food; their generally lighter flavors blend in more easily with the myriad flavors in a Chinese meal. A slightly sweet California Chenin Blanc, New York State Aurora, or German or American Riesling mainly serves as refreshment, without stealing the stage from the food. Gewürztraminer, with its spicy aroma and flavor, is often suggested with dishes with a lot of ginger, garlic, or chile; in this case, the stronger flavor of the wine adds an extra dimension of flavor to the meal.

Red wines have their place with Chinese foods, too. Red-cooked meats taste especially good with a soft, fruity red wine, such as a California or Oregon Pinot Noir or a fine French Beaujolais. Roast duck, whether Cantonese or Peking style, calls for a fuller-flavored red wine, such as a well-aged Cabernet Sauvignon, Merlot, or red Bordeaux.

Sherry is not normally thought of as a table wine, but a dry Spanish Fino can be quite good with steamed fish or stir-fried dishes with black beans. A dry Amontillado or Oloroso can stand in for Shaoxing wine both in the kitchen and at the table.

Soft drinks, especially citrus-flavored ones, sparkling apple cider, and mineral waters are popular non-alcoholic drinks among Chinese-Americans.

PRONUNCIATION GUIDE

This is a slightly simplified guide to modern Chinese (pinyin) spellings. It should help in pronouncing some of the Chinese names in this book and perhaps at your favorite Chinese eatery as well. It does not distinguish between some closely related sounds (*ch* and *q,* for example), but it gives a general idea of the sounds of the standardized letters and their nearest English equivalent.

a: as in "father"
ai: like long *i* in "sigh"
ao: like *ow* in "cow"
b: same as English
c: ts, like Italian *zz* in "pizza"
ch: same as English
d: same as English
e: like *a* in "soda," or *u* in "fun"
ei: like long *a* in "may"
f: same as English
g: like hard *g* in "good"
h: like German *ch* in "Bach"
i: like long *e* in "me"
ia: "yah"
ian: "yen"
iu: like *yo* in "yodel"
j: same as English
k: same as English
l: same as English
m: same as English
n: same as English
ng: same as English
o: like *aw* in "paw"
ong: like *oo* in "good"
ou: like long *o* in "no"
p: same as English
q: like *ch,* but slightly harder
r: same as English
s: same as English
sh: same as English
t: same as English
u: like long *u* in "dune"
ui: "way"
w: same as English
x: like *sh,* but with a *y* sound at the end
y: same as English
z: like *dz* in "adze"
zh: like middle consonant in "vision," or like French *j*

PREPARATION TOOLS

Chinese cooks make do with relatively few hand tools, most of them designed to be used with a wok. The wire strainer, a shallow basket of woven brass wire with a bamboo handle, is used to lift simmered foods out of their liquid, or fried foods out of hot oil. The traditional Chinese spatula is a masterpiece of design; the curved edge of the spatula fits into the curve of the wok for maximum efficiency in stir-frying. The shallow ladle can be used to add liquids to the wok or, in combination with the spatula, to scoop a finished mixture out onto a plate. If possible, look for a ladle and spatula made of stainless steel; the more common rolled-steel variety must be carefully dried and oiled after each washing to prevent rust. (A large metal spoon and a slotted spoon can be used as substitutes for the Chinese spatula and skimmer, but do not use plastic or wooden tools—they will scorch in the heat of the wok.)

An oil can with a long, thin spout is handy for stir-frying. The narrow opening allows you to pour a tablespoon or two of oil in a thin stream around the edge of the wok, coating the sloping sides as it runs down into the center. The best examples come from China and Italy and are nearly identical in design. Don't buy too big a can, however, because it is not a good place for long storage of oil (the original can or bottle, tightly sealed, is better).

Food Processors

Although it will never replace the knife, a food processor has many uses in Chinese cooking. The main thing to remember is that with its great speed, it can overprocess foods in just

a few seconds, so use it carefully. The steel blade does a quick and thorough job of chopping meats and can produce anything from coarsely chopped pork for stir-frying to finely ground stuffings and smooth fish pastes. For the best control, chop meats with on-off pulses, scraping down the bowl several times, until the desired texture is reached.

Noodle and bread doughs can also be mixed in the processor; use the steel blade (not the short plastic dough blade), and do not overprocess. Do the final kneading by hand for the best results.

Fitted with the slicing blade, the processor can be helpful when you are shredding a lot of cabbage or slicing fancy-cut carrots or other decorative vegetables.

However, there are some things the food processor cannot do as well as a knife, such as chopping ginger for stir-fried dishes. Instead of cutting the ginger into discrete little bits, the machine smashes and tears it, ruining the texture and spraying the aromatic juice all over the inside of the work bowl. Garlic, shallots, and green onions are also better cut by hand than by machine.

Graters and Grinders

A few recipes call for grated ginger, particularly in sauces where the ginger juice flavors a liquid mixture. The best graters for this purpose are Japanese, with a series of fine teeth that rake the flesh off the fibers. The finest side of a box grater also works, although it is harder to clean. Do not, however, use grated ginger as a substitute for minced, as the texture will be all wrong.

Chinese cooking does not use many ground spices, but for the few recipes of this type (such as Sichuan Pepper Salt, page 34) an electric spice grinder is very handy. A mortar and pestle or a hand-cranked spice mill work just as well.

COOKING EQUIPMENT

Chinese cooking requires little in the way of specialized tools and equipment. The recipes in this book can be prepared with the pots, pans, and other equipment found in a typical home kitchen. However, there are certain designs that the Chinese have perfected over several thousand years.

The Wok

The most famous symbol of Chinese cooking is the wok, and it is hard to imagine a more versatile or better-designed piece of cookware. Its round bottom allows foods to be stir-fried or deep-fried with a minimum of oil. A steel or cast iron wok is an excellent conductor of heat, making it possible to cook over a very small fire. With a cover and a steaming rack or basket, the wok becomes a steamer for everything from whole birds and fish to bite-sized pastries. You can simmer, braise, and even smoke foods in a wok. Once you become used to cooking in a wok, you may find it indispensable, and not just for Chinese cooking; it is equally useful for anything from an Italian pasta sauce to an Indian curry.

Woks are available in many designs and materials. The traditional shape is round bottomed, for cooking over a gas flame (originally a charcoal brazier). Cooks with electric ranges should use a flat-bottomed wok for more efficient heating. A wok may have two metal loops as handles, two similar handles trimmed with wood, or one long wooden handle with or without a handle on the opposite side. A long handle is useful, especially for stir-frying, as it allows you to lift the wok with one hand, and shovel with the other, as you pour the contents out onto the serving platter.

The best material for woks is 14-gauge spun steel, about 5/64 inch thick. It is light enough for easy handling but heavy enough to conduct heat well. Cast iron is also traditional, but many home cooks find it too heavy. Other materials have definite disadvantages. Nonstick surfaces may make cleaning easier, but they do not allow foods to brown as well as steel or iron surfaces do. Stainless steel is pretty, but it conducts heat poorly, and food tends to stick to it. Anodized aluminum performs well but is very expensive.

Woks come in all sizes, from 12 to 30 inches in diameter. The 14-inch size is the most common for home use and is included in the standard wok sets sold in most cookware and department stores. This is a good compromise size, especially if you have only one wok. However, if your stove-top space permits, a 16-inch or larger wok will make it much easier to cook a whole fish or duck. An ideal home set would include a 16-inch round-bottomed wok with metal handles (for cooking large items and frying in quantity) and a 12- or 14-inch long-handled wok (for most stir-fried dishes).

Among the essential wok accessories (included in most wok sets) are a wok ring, a cover, and a Chinese-style wire strainer, ladle, and spatula. The ring, made of perforated metal, holds a round-bottomed wok steady over the fire. Some manufacturers of electric ranges now offer a replacement burner coil especially for round-bottomed woks, combining a ring with concave heating coils that match the shape of the wok. The cover should be a high dome, rather like a mirror image of the wok, to accommodate large items, such as steamed fish.

Optional wok accessories include steaming racks and bamboo steaming baskets (see Steaming, page 78), wire draining racks for fried foods (see page 51), bamboo cleaning brushes, and extralong chopsticks for stirring while food cooks.

ABOUT SPELLING

Trying to render Chinese words in English can be a confusing matter. First, there are many regional dialects. The speech of the capital (Mandarin Chinese) is now the official language of the whole country, but many millions of people in southern China and abroad speak Cantonese, and millions more speak other dialects. Although all the dialects use the same written characters to represent words, the same word may be pronounced quite differently. Thus, the steamed pork dumplings on page 121 are known as *shao mai* in Mandarin and *siu mi* in Cantonese. The cabbage known as *bok choy* in the south is pronounced *pak tsai* in the north.

Another problem lies in translating Chinese sounds into Roman letters. Various systems have been used over the years. The city in eastern China known on many maps as Tsingtao is spelled Ch'ingtao on others; and under the pinyin system adopted by the People's Republic in the 1950s, the spelling is Qingdao. All of these are attempts to "accurately" reflect the pronunciation *ching-dow*. On the whole, pinyin is easier to use once you learn its rules. There is no doubt that Beijing is a better phonetic representation of the name of the capital than the old spelling Peking. (For a pronunciation guide to pinyin, see the opposite page.) In this book, we use the pinyin spellings for place names and—except for the some of the most common restaurant dishes—we generally avoid using Chinese names for foods.

HOW TO USE CHOPSTICKS

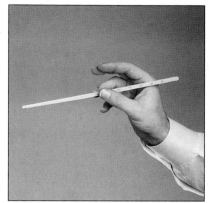

1. Personal styles vary. Pictured is a four-finger method. Hold one chopstick in crook between thumb and forefinger, braced firmly against ring finger. This one does not move.

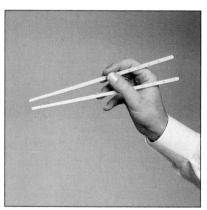

2. Grasp other chopstick between thumb and first two fingers, like a pencil. Move this one up and down to grasp foods.

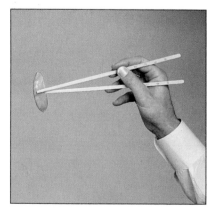

3. For best control, keep tips of chopsticks even.

Seasoning the Wok

Like a cast-iron skillet or griddle, a steel wok must be carefully seasoned. A well-seasoned wok can cook foods in the tiniest amount of oil without sticking, yet it "grips" the food during cooking for good browning in a way no nonstick coated surface can.

Before using a brand new wok, wash it well with detergent and a scouring pad to remove the protective coating of mineral oil. This should be the last time you wash it with detergent! Dry the wok well, then place it on a burner over medium-high heat. When the metal has dried out thoroughly and gets a bluish haze in the middle, turn off the heat and pour in 2 to 3 tablespoons of cooking oil in a thin stream around the edge of the pan. Let the wok cool slightly, then rub the oil around all over the inside with several thicknesses of paper towels. Rub until all the oil is absorbed and the towel picks up a gray stain from the metal. Heat again, add a little more oil, and wipe away the oil with another clean towel. Repeat with two or three more coats of oil, or until the towel comes out clean.

Once the wok has been seasoned, the surface must still be carefully maintained. After each use, wash it immediately with hot water. If any scrubbing is necessary, use a sponge, soft-bristled plastic brush, or plastic scrubbing pad, but never anything more abrasive. (The bamboo wok brushes sold with some wok sets don't work very well.) Wipe the wok dry, return it to the heat for a minute to dry further, and rub it with a little oil. Eventually, the wok will develop a thin black coating inside and out, and you will find its cooking qualities getting better and better.

Unfortunately, some uses of the wok take away this carefully preserved finish. Steaming is especially hard on the oil coating, as are salt-buried cooking and smoking. Whenever the finish is stripped by one of these methods or by neglect (such as leaving it full of water in the sink), it will have to be reseasoned. Deep-frying, on the other hand, is one of the best ways to build the patina.

TABLEWARE

The typical Chinese place setting for an informal family meal consists of a pair of chopsticks, a bowl for rice or other *fan*, a smaller soup bowl, a soup spoon, and a small saucer for bones. Everyone helps themselves to items from the platters (usually with their chopsticks, sometimes with serving spoons), dishing a morsel or two into their rice bowls before eating it with chopsticks and putting the bones on their bone dishes.

A more formal setting may include individual plates, fancy chopstick rests, tiny bowls for condiments and dipping sauces, and even individual serving spoons. At a formal banquet, rice is not served until the end, so the dishes are eaten from the plate.

In either setting, dishes are served on an assortment of round and oval platters of various sizes. Soup is typically served in a covered tureen, and rice in a large, covered bowl. Tea is generally served after the meal, in small cups without handles.

Chinese food looks most authentic served on Chinese porcelain dishes, with their fancy borders decorated with dragons, good-luck characters, or geometric patterns. Imported Chinese tableware can be quite inexpensive in Chinese markets and import specialty stores. Of course, your Chinese cooking will taste just as good served from any attractive "china."

Chopsticks

Thousands of years before Westerners began eating with forks, the Chinese had mastered the use of chopsticks. The design of these ingenious eating implements has changed little since they evolved from simple stirring sticks a few thousand years ago. Whether made of plain or lacquered wood, bamboo, plastic, silver, or ivory, they remain the best way to eat Chinese food.

Chinese chopsticks taper only slightly from the handle to the end. Beginners might find the more slender Japanese variety easier to handle. Unfinished wood or bamboo also grips the food better than a highly polished lacquered surface.

It is perfectly good Chinese table manners to lift a bowl of rice or noodles near to the mouth and shovel the food into the mouth with the chopsticks. Most Westerners, however, prefer to lift the food out of the bowl or plate. Either method works.

To eat chicken, spareribs, or other meats with bones, either hold the morsel with chopsticks and nibble the meat off the bones, or take the whole thing into the mouth and work the bones free with the teeth and tongue. Again, Eastern and Western etiquette differ on how to remove the bones from one's mouth; Chinese technique is to spit the bones out directly into the bone dish, but Western diners may prefer to transfer them with chopsticks or the soup spoon. Each method is equally polite in its place; let the situation be your guide.

Chopsticks are as useful in the kitchen as at the table. Plain, undecorated wooden chopsticks can be used to stir a dough, mix a cornstarch solution before adding it to the wok, pull a noodle from the cooking pot for tasting, dip foods in a frying batter, or retrieve something from the frying oil. Most wok sets include a pair of long cooking chopsticks, or you can find them in cookware shops and Asian grocery stores.

Chinese tableware can be plain or fancy, but the basic place setting is the same for most meals— chopsticks, a soup bowl and spoon, a larger bowl for rice, small dishes for dipping sauces, and a small plate for bones. Porcelain soup spoons are authentic but optional. Banquets and other fancy meals call for a large plate and decorative chopstick rests.

Three knives can handle all the cutting chores in Chinese cooking: a heavy-bladed Chinese knife suitable for use as a cleaver; a lighter version for slicing, mincing, and chopping vegetables and boned meats; and a paring knife for peeling and other delicate work.

KNIVES

Good cooking begins with good cutting. Nowhere is this more true than in the Chinese kitchen. Whatever the food, whatever the cooking method, there is an appropriate way of cutting that will ensure the best results. Cutting foods into uniform-sized pieces ensures that they will cook at the same rate, a necessity in high-speed stir-frying as well as in slow braising.

Typically, the Chinese have taken this simple necessity and raised it to the level of art. A skillful Chinese cook can quickly reduce an assortment of vegetables and meats to just the right size, exposing just the right amount of surface area to cook perfectly, and they will be pretty to look at as well.

Three basic types of knives will cover nearly any cutting task in Chinese cooking: a large-bladed vegetable knife, a heavy cleaver, and a small-bladed paring or utility knife. Before examining each of them in detail, a few general remarks on Chinese knives are in order.

The typical Chinese knife, regardless of its use, has a large, rectangular blade and looks vaguely like a Western meat cleaver. For this reason, the whole range of Chinese knives, from lightweight vegetable knives to extraheavy, bone-chopping cleavers, tend to be lumped together under the name "Chinese cleaver." But the name is misleading; only the heaviest of these knives are cleavers in the Western sense (that is, knives built to chop through bones). The lighter versions are strictly for cutting up vegetables and boneless meats.

To determine the suitability of a Chinese knife for a given task, look for a number imprinted on the blade; the higher the number, the smaller and lighter the knife. A number 1 Chinese knife can chop poultry bones or pork ribs with ease, but its thick blade and heavy weight make it more difficult to use for precise vegetable cutting. On the other hand, using a number 2, 3, or 4 knife to chop through bones will undoubtedly put nicks or dents in the cutting edge.

Materials and construction of Chinese-style knives vary. Some have stainless steel blades, others have blades of carbon steel. Carbon-steel blades are somewhat easier to sharpen and to keep sharp, but they have a major disadvantage: acid fruits and certain vegetables such as ginger, garlic, and onions will react chemically with the metal, producing discoloration and flavor changes. Fortunately, most Chinese- and Western-made knives are now available with stainless steel blades.

Most Chinese knives have wooden handles, but in some cases the handle is a hollow extension of the same piece of steel as the blade. Wooden handles are often grooved or wrapped with wire for a better grip. Choose whichever handle style feels best in your hand.

The Vegetable Knife

Unless otherwise specified, the cutting instructions on the following pages and throughout this book are for a vegetable knife. This can be either a medium-weight Chinese knife or its nearest Western equivalent, the French chef's knife. The ideal Chinese vegetable knife is a number 3 or 4, preferably with a stainless steel blade. Choose the size that feels most comfortable in your hand, but if in doubt, go with the larger knife; with practice you will find the extra size and weight working for you.

Although a large vegetable knife may feel unwieldy at first, you may soon find it indispensable. Not only is it good for slicing, dicing, and mincing, but its broad side can be used to smash garlic cloves or ginger to a pulp or to pound chicken breasts to translucent thinness. The blade is also handy for scooping up whatever you have just cut, from a bit of minced ginger to a pile of sliced celery, and transferring it to the wok. Even the dull back edge of the blade is used for certain techniques (see Sizzling Rice Soup, page 66), and some cooks use the end of the handle as a pestle for grinding Sichuan peppercorns and other spices.

The Cleaver

For cutting meats and poultry through the bone, you will need a heavier, sturdier blade than your vegetable knife. Choose either a number 1 knife or an even heavier, thicker-bladed cleaver with no number on the blade. Heavy cleavers are ground differently from vegetable knives: Whereas the blade of a vegetable knife is flat-ground, with a constant taper from the top to the cutting edge, the cleaver blade tapers slowly from the top to within an inch or so of the edge and then tapers quickly to the cutting edge. The result, technically known as a roll grind, is an edge that is not as fine as that of the vegetable knife but is capable of hacking through bones without denting or cracking. A cleaver can be used for coarse chopping of meats and vegetables, but its bulkier blade makes precise work, especially thin slicing, more difficult.

The Paring Knife

Some cutting tasks, such as peeling ginger, deveining shrimp, and making fancy decorative cuts, require a smaller, lighter knife. A Western-style paring knife is ideal. Just because this is a small knife, however, don't try to save money by buying a cheap one; a good paring knife from a reputable German, French, or American manufacturer will probably cost as much as your Chinese vegetable knife. It will be worth every penny of the cost, however, as it will take and hold an edge better than a cheap knife.

Sharpening

A sharp edge is an absolute necessity, and not only for good cutting. It is also a matter of safety; one of the easiest ways to cut yourself is by trying to force a cut with a dull knife.

The easiest and best way to maintain a sharp edge on a Chinese knife (or any knife for that matter) is with a sharpening steel. If you don't already own a steel, buy one and learn to use it; it will save you time, money, and frustration. The ideal steel is at least 12 inches long, not counting the handle, with a smooth or very finely ridged surface. The steel does not remove any metal from the edge, as a whetstone does; rather, it realigns the cutting edge to keep it razor sharp. Use the steel every time you bring out your knife and it will hardly ever need to be sharpened on a stone or reground.

To sharpen a Chinese knife with a steel, hold the steel vertically, with the tip resting on the cutting board. Place the heel of the blade against the steel near the top, with the blade making a 15- to 20-degree angle with the steel. (Too wide an angle dulls the edge; too narrow an angle will produce a brittle, fragile edge that dulls easily with use.) Maintaining gentle sideways pressure against the steel, swing the blade downward, drawing the length of the cutting edge across the steel. Repeat on the other side of the steel. Alternate sides, making 10 or 12 strokes in all.

Cutting Surfaces

With so much chopping, slicing, and mincing going on, the cutting surface is almost as important as the knife. The cutting surface must be soft enough to cushion the edge of the blade so that it will not dull the knife, but hard enough to resist splintering or otherwise disintegrating into the food. Wood is the favorite cutting surface of most cooks, and the traditional Chinese "chopping block" is simply a slice of a hardwood tree. Laminated hardwood cutting boards and end-grain "butcher blocks" are both excellent choices.

Wooden boards have some disadvantages, however. They require a lot of care, including periodic scraping and oiling. They also tend to absorb odors from foods and are harder to sterilize and deodorize than nonporous materials. For this reason, some cooks prefer a synthetic cutting surface for cutting up meats, poultry, and especially seafood. The best synthetic boards are made of a dense, opaque white polycarbonate and have a slightly uneven surface that "gives" under the knife blade much as wood does. They are easy to clean with dishwashing detergent (which should never be used on a wooden board). Do not confuse these boards with decorative boards of shiny, clear plastic or any other hard surface, which will dull knives.

Whether you use a wood or synthetic cutting board, choose the largest size that will easily fit your work space. Nothing is more frustrating than trying to cut a lot of things on a tiny cutting board.

CUTTING TECHNIQUES

In the following techniques, the "knife hand" is used to mean the knife-holding hand, and the "other hand" the one that holds the food to be cut. Although they are illustrated with a Chinese vegetable knife, a French chef's knife or Japanese vegetable knife will also work.

Work slowly at first until you get the hang of each technique; speed will come along naturally. The important thing is to learn safe and efficient cutting habits. Give yourself plenty of room to work, stand in a comfortable position, relax, and focus entirely on the task at hand; you will find yourself cutting quickly and with minimum effort.

Hand Position

Holding food for safe and precise cutting is mostly a matter of keeping your fingers out of the way of the blade. For most cutting tasks, this means holding the food against the board with the fingertips of the holding hand curled back away from the blade. The blade then rides against the curved knuckles to guide the cut. As long as you do not lift the blade above the level of the knuckles and do not straighten out the fingers, there is no way that you can cut yourself in this position.

The knife-hand position depends upon the task. For precise cutting, grip the knife handle close to the blade, with the thumb and forefinger grasping the blade itself. There are two basic blade positions: Either rest the tip of the knife on the board and slice with a rocking motion, or lift the entire blade and, holding the edge parallel to the board, slice with a downward and forward motion. The former method allows more control, the latter more speed. For other grips, see "Chopping" and "Cleaver Chopping," on page 18.

Slicing

Whether you are making thick or thin slices, crosswise or diagonal, the procedure is the same. Hold the ingredient with the fingers curled back and the knuckles one slice-thickness back from the edge. Slice, using the knuckles to guide the blade, and then move the fingers back along the food (or push the food forward with the thumb) to get into position for the next slice.

Slant-Cutting and Roll-Cutting

These are two typical Chinese variations of slicing, both designed to increase the surface area of the cut pieces. Slant-cutting, used mainly for slender vegetables like celery and bok choy stalks, is done either by cutting straight down with the knife held at an angle across the food or by holding the knife at an angle away from vertical. Choose whichever feels more natural to you.

Roll-cutting is a technique for cutting cylindrical vegetables, such as carrots and asparagus. Slice off one end at about a 45-degree angle. Roll the vegetable a quarter turn and slice again to cut off as long a piece as desired. Continue turning the vegetable a quarter turn with each cut. The angles need not be precise; part of the charm of roll-cut vegetables is their irregular shape.

Smashing

To crush garlic, ginger, or green onions prior to chopping, or to release their juices into a marinade, smack them smartly with the broad side of the blade. Another method is to place the knife flat on top and then pound it with your fist.

Shredding and Julienne-Cutting

To cut food into fine shreds or larger "matchsticks," first cut the ingredient into slices of the desired length and thickness. Carrots and other slender vegetables may have to be slant-cut to achieve the right length. Stack the slices, overlapped slightly like shingles, and slice down through the stack lengthwise, cutting the slices into sticks that are square in cross section. Shreds are very fine julienne pieces, about 1/16 inch thick; matchsticks are twice as thick.

Note When slicing or shredding ginger, be sure to slice first across the grain; otherwise, the pieces may be unpleasantly fibrous.

To shred green onions, first slice them into the desired length. Slit the white and pale green sections lengthwise, but do not cut all the way through. Open halves like a book and cut lengthwise into thin shreds. To shred the hollow green tops, simply bundle them together under the fingertips of the left hand and carefully slice the bundle into shreds.

Precise cutting is essential to Chinese cooking. Shredding each vegetable in Mu Shu Pork (see page 45) to the appropriate size ensures even cooking.

Dicing and Mincing

These two terms refer to the same process but differ in the size of the cut: Diced means cut into cubes of ¼ to ½ inch; minced, about 1/16 inch; finely diced is somewhere in between. First, cut the ingredient into shreds or matchsticks of the desired thickness, as described above. Then gather the sticks in a bundle and cut across into uniform cubes.

Garlic, onion, and shallot are minced by a slightly different method. First peel, leaving the root end intact, and then split in half lengthwise. Place the cut side down on the board, and, holding the knife horizontally, make one or more cuts parallel to the cutting board, almost to the root end. Next, make a series of vertical lengthwise cuts of the desired thickness. Then slice across the cuts toward the root end to produce cubes. Discard the root end.

Chopping

Sometimes uniform cubes are not necessary. For example, in a dish such as Spicy Bean Sauce Noodles (see page 110), random-sized bits of ginger and garlic provide texture as well as flavor to the sauce. To save time, these ingredients can be chopped rather than minced or diced. Place a pile of peeled garlic cloves or ginger slices on the board. Grip the knife a little farther out on the handle than for slicing. Use the other hand to press the tip of the knife down against the board and chop with a rocking motion, pivoting the knife back and forth over the food. Chop to the desired size, scraping the pile together occasionally.

Cleaver Chopping

With a cleaver or a heavier vegetable knife, it is easy to chop meats to any texture, from rough cubes to a fine paste. Start by dicing the meat, and then change to a chopping grip (knife hand well back on the handle, thumb on top or on side). Swing from the wrist for maximum chopping efficiency. With a good, heavy

cleaver, not much downward force is really necessary; it is more a matter of lifting the knife and letting it fall. The other hand is not involved in this type of chopping, unless it is to hold a second cleaver to speed up the operation (see next paragraph). Stop every once in a while to scrape the pile of pieces back together.

A variation on this technique is to use two knives, one in each hand. Ideally, they should be nearly the same size and weight; if they are mismatched, wield the heavier knife with your stronger hand. Chop alternately, as if doing a slow drum roll.

To chop through bones, as in cutting a chicken into serving pieces or chopping up spareribs for braising, hold the knife as above. However, it may be necessary to hold the food with the other hand. For safety's sake, keep your hand holding the food as far away from where you will cut as possible. When you get to the last couple of inches, just place the food on the board, get your hand out of the way, take aim, and chop.

Cutting Up Poultry

Chicken may be disjointed with a Chinese cleaver or a boning knife. The following steps also apply to whole ducks or any other type of poultry, from squab to turkey.

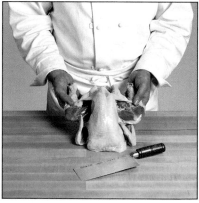

Pick up chicken with both hands, breast side up. Spread legs outward to pop the hip joints free.

Cut through skin between leg and breast. Turn chicken on its side, and cut leg free, along with meat from back. (If you will be using the back, leave more meat attached to back.)

Pull wing away from body, and cut away from breast. Do not cut too deeply into breast meat. Repeat with other leg and wing.

Hold chicken by tip of breastbone, and cut through ribs to separate breast from back. Pull or chop breast free from back at base of wishbone.

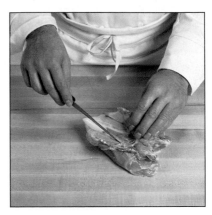

Boning the Breast

Remove skin. Place breast skin side down. With tip of knife, cut through membrane covering breastbone.

Pick up breast with both hands and press back on ribs to break them away from breastbone, which will pop out. Pull out breastbone, including cartilage.

With short cuts, using tip of knife, cut away ribs as close to bone as possible. *Or:* Slip fingers between ribs and meat and work meat free from bones. Work wishbone free with fingers.

Split breast in half, removing tough membranes lying along breastbone. Locate white tendon on smaller muscle of each half. Place tendon side down on board and hold end with a fingernail. With knife held vertically, scrape from end of tendon inward, scraping meat away from tendon.

Cutting for Braising

To cut a chicken into braising pieces (1- to 2-inch pieces with bones), first disjoint the bird as instructed above. Remove excess fat from the cavity and neck area. Remove the kidneys— the spongy organs along the backbone near the tail end. Rinse well.

Separate legs and wings from body. Hold a leg by the end of the drumstick, as far from cutting point as possible. Grasp cleaver with the chopping grip (see page 18). Lift blade and chop down through thigh bone with a firm, decisive blow. The knife should cut cleanly through the bone without shattering it. Cut thigh and drumstick into two or three pieces each. For safety's sake, keep your holding hand as far away from where you will cut as possible.

19

Hold wings by tips and cut upper and middle joints into two pieces each. Leave tip whole, for decoration.

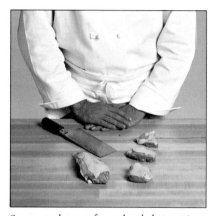

Separate breast from back by cutting through ribs. Split breast in half lengthwise, and then chop each breast half into three or four pieces, leaving the skin attached.

Chop along one side of backbone to split the back in half; leave backbone attached to other side. Chop each back half crosswise into four or five small pieces.

To cut up cooked poultry Chinese style, use the same process. For the best presentation, arrange the cut pieces on the serving platter as soon as they are cut. Start with the legs and place them at one end of an oval platter, then cut and arrange the wings at the other end. Traditional Chinese cooks place the head and tail at either end of the platter, but this is optional. Put the back pieces into the center, topped by the breast pieces, skin side up. This step-by-step approach is much easier than cutting up the whole bird and then trying to reassemble the pieces of the puzzle!

Cutting Fish

Although it may seem an unwieldy tool for the purpose, the Chinese knife does a good job of filleting fish.

Starting on left side of fish, make a diagonal cut just behind gill opening to separate fillet from head.

Turn fish tail toward you. Holding the knife horizontally, cut along back side just above fins. With one or two long, shallow cuts, cut half of fillet away from bones, peeling it back gently as you go.

Continue cutting and peeling back fillet until ribs show on belly side. Cut through tiny pin bones, then along outside of rib cage, not through ribs. Cut through skin on belly side, then toward tail to free one fillet. Repeat first three steps on other side of fish.

To skin fillets, place skin side down on board. Hold skin down with fingernails. Holding knife at a 15- to 20-degree angle from horizontal, cut between meat and skin with one long, smooth motion, as if shaving the inside of the skin.

Preparing a Whole Fish

A whole fish, whether steamed, fried, or braised, is always an impressive dish, and is the traditional end to a Chinese banquet. For most purposes, a 1- to 3-pound fish is the most convenient size. The main consideration is what will fit your wok or steamer and serving platter.

Have fish cleaned and scaled, leaving head and tail. Cut open belly cavity. Pull away gills and internal organs. Look for two strips of red tissue lying along the backbone; if present, cut them open with tip of knife. Rinse cavity well under running water until no traces of bloody tissues remain.

Score both sides of fish with diagonal cuts almost to the bone, 1 to 2 inches apart. This scoring method both speeds the cooking time and allows the seasonings to better penetrate the fish.

If you want to serve a steamed fish "swimming" on the platter (belly side down), cut back from cavity toward tail along one side of bones. Spread the cut open and arrange fish upright on the steaming plate.

Preparing Shrimp

For maximum flavor, cook and serve shrimp in the shell.

To devein unpeeled shrimp, use a small knife to cut outward through the shell along the back, exposing the vein.

Butterflying shrimp increases their surface area and reduces cooking time. Peel shrimp, leaving tail fins attached. Cut almost through tail from back to underside. Remove vein and unfold shrimp.

Larger shrimp can be peeled and split entirely in half lengthwise, producing two pieces that curl attractively when cooked.

Preparing Crab

Use this method for cutting up freshly killed live crabs or cooked crabs.

Kill and clean crab as described in the recipe for Steamed Crab on page 81. Split cleaned body in half down the middle.

Cut between legs to separate each half into five pieces, each attached to a leg or claw. Illustrated here with Dungeness crab, the same technique works with smaller varieties such as the eastern blue crab.

Crack each section of leg and claw with a mallet or with the dull back edge of a cleaver.

Cucumber fans, chrysanthemums
of daikon radish, and
orange-peel roses are just some
of the fancy garnishes used
to dress up Chinese dishes.

Chinese cooking gets its flavor from ingredients both familiar and exotic. The most important of these are described in the following pages.

Ingredients, Condiments & Sauces

The Chinese cook, like successful cooks everywhere, relies on good basic ingredients. Here is a guide to the fresh, canned, dried, and preserved foods that you will need to prepare authentic Chinese dishes, as well as recipes for basic condiments and sauces. Most of the ingredients are familiar items that can be found in supermarkets everywhere. Some are more exotic and may require a trip to Chinatown or a specialty food shop, or you may need to order them by mail. Tips on shopping and mail-order sources are included.

THE CHINESE PANTRY

A well-stocked Chinese grocery can contain enough exotic ingredients for a lifetime of culinary exploration. Many of these canned, dried, and packaged ingredients are also available in supermarkets and gourmet shops, or by mail order (see page 37). To get you started, here is a guide to the most common ingredients used in the recipes in this book.

Bamboo Shoots The edible shoots of large bamboo plants give crunch and a slightly sweet flavor to stir-fried and other dishes. They are available in cans—and sometimes fresh—in Chinese markets (see page 37). Drain and discard canning liquid, and if a canned flavor persists, blanch briefly in fresh water before using. Store in an air-tight container and covered with fresh water in the refrigerator.

Bean Curd See Tofu.

Black Beans, Fermented and Salted Before there was soy sauce, miso, or any other prepared bean sauce, the Chinese were preserving soybeans by first fermenting and then salting them. This ancient food is still used today in southern Chinese cooking, especially in sauces for fish and shellfish. These soft black beans, flecked with salt crystals, are sold in Chinese groceries in cans or small bags usually labeled "salted black beans." Do not confuse them with the uncooked variety, which is sold in similar packages. Typically, the beans are chopped and soaked in a little wine before being added to a sauce. They generally provide all the salt the dish needs.

Black Mushrooms, Dried Also known by their Japanese name, *shiitake*, these mushrooms are one of the most important ingredients in East Asian cooking. They have a broad flat cap, a short stem, and a fine meaty flavor. Asian markets carry several grades; the best (and the most expensive, naturally) have a lacy system of cracks on the surface of the brown cap, showing the creamy flesh underneath. To get the best price, buy them in bulk if at all possible. Dried black mushrooms keep well in a cool, dry place. To use, soak in warm water until soft, then drain and discard the tough stems. If the liquid is not used in the dish, save it for soups or stocks.

Note The fresh shiitake mushrooms now being raised commercially in North America do not have the depth of flavor of the imported dried variety and should not be used as a substitute. They are very good, however, in place of fresh mushrooms.

Chiles Like peanuts and tomatoes, hot chile peppers were imported from the New World via the West only a few centuries ago, and, therefore, are a fairly recent addition to Chinese cuisine. They have become an essential ingredient in the cooking of western and northern China, and are used to a lesser degree in other parts of the country.

Of the chiles available in this country, the fresh and dried versions of the small, hot *chile serrano* are the most useful in Chinese cooking. Fresh serranos—green or sometimes red, 2 to 3 inches long and up to ½ inch thick—are available in most supermarkets, especially where there is a Latin or Asian population. Fresh jalapeño chiles are somewhat larger but otherwise interchangeable. The ripened and dried version of the serrano is the familiar small, dried red chili of supermarket spice racks; but it is cheaper to buy it in bulk.

Caution Be careful in handling any chiles, fresh or dried. The flesh, seeds, and especially the ribs or veins contain an irritating substance called capsaicin. The potency can be deceptive because there is a delayed reaction between contact and sensation. Do not touch your face, especially your eyes or mouth, while working with chiles. When finished wash your hands (and knives and other tools) thoroughly with soap and water. If your skin is especially sensitive, or if you will be working with many chiles, wear rubber or plastic gloves.

Chile Oil A flavoring oil rather than a cooking oil, this condiment is made by heating dried chiles in peanut or sesame oil and steeping them for several hours or days. Serve with dim sum and noodle dishes.

Chinese Sausage This firm, slender, slightly sweet sausage is made mainly of pork liver. It is sold in packages or loose in pairs tied together with a string. Keeps well under refrigeration or frozen.

Cloud Ears An edible fungus, these are also known as "tree ears," "wood ears," "black fungus," and, as translated on some package labels, "dehydrated vegetable." Cloud ears are used mainly for their crunchy yet gelatinous texture in Chinese soups and stir-fried dishes. Like many other Chinese products, they come in different types and grades. The best type is sold in packages of small, irregular pieces, each less than an inch across, deep brown on top and medium brown on the underside. The other common form—black on top and pale gray underneath—is much larger and tougher, even after soaking.

Five-Spice Powder This is a typical Chinese spice blend, used especially for meats and poultry. Five-spice blends vary and may contain six or seven spices. Packaged blends are available in Chinese markets, or you can make your own (page 34).

Ham, Smithfield In Chinese cooking, ham is used more as a seasoning than as a meat ingredient. Unless otherwise specified, use Smithfield ham from Virginia (the closest equivalent to the famous Yunnan ham of China) or another fine dry-cured country ham. Most recipes call for slicing the ham thinly and soaking it in a little water to remove some of the salt. Some Chinese markets sell Smithfield ham in pieces, so it is not necessary to buy a whole ham. Store cut pieces in the refrigerator.

Some of the dried, preserved, and packaged foods used in this book may already be in your pantry; others will require a trip to a Chinese market.

DRY YOUR OWN ORANGE PEEL

1. *Wash and peel an orange or tangerine. Cut or tear peel into pieces roughly 1 by 3 inches.*

2. *Place pieces of peel, colored side down, near edge of cutting board. Pare away white pith with a vegetable peeler using a sawing motion, until orange color shows through.*

3. *Dry thoroughly on a cake rack and store in a tightly sealed jar. Keeps indefinitely.*

Hoisin Sauce Sweetened and spiced soybean sauce is popular as both a condiment and a sauce ingredient in northern China. *Hoisin* sauce is sometimes served with Peking Duck in Chinese restaurants. Available in jars and cans, it keeps well in the refrigerator, or a little less well at room temperature.

Lily Buds The dried, unopened buds of a tiger lily are also known as "golden needles." Soaked in water and drained, they add a pleasant texture and slightly tart and tealike flavor to certain Chinese dishes, especially Hot and Sour Soup (page 67) and Mu Shu Pork (page 45).

Monosodium Glutamate (MSG) As a flavor enhancer, MSG is used in many processed foods and by some cooks (Accent is a common brand). Although MSG is a naturally occurring substance, there is concern about health risks associated with its use. Individual sensitivity to MSG varies. Some people experience an allergylike reaction to MSG—known as "the Chinese restaurant syndrome"—because of the all-too-common restaurant practice of using MSG as a flavor stretcher. Others find MSG leaves a metallic aftertaste; it certainly is high in sodium. None of the recipes in this book call for MSG.

Mushrooms In addition to the familiar cultivated button mushroom and the dried black mushroom (see page 26), there are several types of mushrooms available in specialty markets that are useful in Chinese cooking. The slender Japanese *enokitake*, which can be bought fresh in small bags, has a delicate flavor and crunchy texture that make it especially good in clear soups. Both the fresh shiitake and the pale gray oyster mushroom, with its off-center stem, are good in stir-fried dishes.

Another variety, the small, bulb-stemmed straw mushroom, is available in cans from China. It has a mild flavor similar to that of commercial mushrooms, but its unusual shape makes it an interesting addition to soups and stir-fried dishes.

Oils Chinese frying and stir-frying demand a mild or neutral-tasting vegetable oil that can stand high heat. Peanut oil, with its high smoking point and fine flavor, is the first choice, but cottonseed oil is often used for economy. Other vegetable oils such as corn, safflower, sunflower, or soybean are also suitable. Recipes in this book do not specify the type of oil; the choice up is to the cook. See Sesame Oil and Chile Oil.

Orange Peel, Dried An aromatic ingredient in many southern Chinese dishes, dried orange or tangerine peel is available in packages in Chinese groceries.

Oyster Sauce This thick, brown extract of salted oysters is used mainly in southern China to flavor meat and vegetable dishes. Brands vary in quality and price, but the best ones are worth the extra cost.

Plum Sauce A sweet-spicy sauce of yellow plums flavored with chile, garlic, and vinegar, plum sauce is used as a table condiment for roast pork or duck, and occasionally in cooking. Koon Chun is a widely available brand from Hong Kong. Recipes for homemade plum sauce appear on page 34.

Salt The recipes in this book were developed using kosher salt, a coarse, flaky, noniodized salt with a milder flavor than standard table salt. When a recipe specifies kosher salt, do not use another type. In other recipes table salt or sea salt may be used but start with *half* the amount called for in the recipe and adjust to taste.

Sesame Oil Not to be confused with the light-colored sesame oil sold in health-food stores, Chinese-style sesame oil is a highly aromatic oil pressed from toasted sesame seeds. Use in small quantities as a flavoring and perfuming agent, not as a cooking oil. It is expensive, but a little goes a long way. Less expensive blends of sesame oil are, not surprisingly, less flavorful. Store sesame oil in a cool, dark place or in the refrigerator, as it tends to become rancid with exposure to heat and light.

Shaoxing (Shao Hsing) Wine This medium-brown rice wine from the city of Shaoxing, eastern China, is made similarly to sake, the Japanese rice wine, but is darker and more full-flavored. Sake should not be used as a substitute. If substitution is necessary, use a good dry but full-bodied sherry, preferably a Spanish dry Oloroso. Shaoxing is mostly used as an ingredient in marinades and sauces, especially in the "red-cooked" dishes of eastern China, but it can be served as a beverage as well (see What to Drink With Chinese Food, page 9).

Shrimp, Dried Tiny dried shrimp are a common feature of Asian and Latin markets. Minced or ground, they are used in some Chinese dishes for flavor and texture. They have a powerful odor when raw, but it disappears with soaking and cooking, leaving a delicious flavor. Store in a sealed jar at room temperature.

Sichuan Peppercorns (fagara, Chinese pepper) Not a true pepper, but the seeds of a prickly ash tree, these are used as a spice in Chinese cooking. The flavor is distinctive but only vaguely pepperlike, more numbing than hot. Available in small packets in Chinese markets, usually labeled "dried Chinese pepper." The whole brown peppercorns are usually toasted in a dry skillet before grinding.

Soy Sauce Soy sauces can be classified in many ways—light or dark, thin or thick, sweet or unsweetened.

For the recipes in this book, "soy sauce" without any other label refers to a Japanese-style light or thin soy sauce, such as the nationally available Kikkoman brand. "Dark soy sauce" covers most Chinese soy sauces (Superior is a good brand); these are noticeably saltier, so they should be used in smaller quantities. A few recipes call for black soy sauce, a thicker, saltier, darker Chinese sauce with a touch of molasses. Koon Chun is a widely distributed brand from Hong Kong.

Note Real soy sauce is a fermented product of soybeans, wheat, water, and salt. Tamari (available in health-food stores) is essentially the same but without the wheat. Avoid the synthetic soy sauces made from hydrolyzed soy protein, most of which are sold under familiar Chinese-sounding brand names.

Star Anise This spice, though unrelated to anise, has a similar licorice flavor. The seed pods resemble eight-point stars, each point containing one seed. Whether a recipe calls for whole pods or a certain number of points, it means both the seeds and their hard covering. Essential to five-spice powder and Chinese red-cooked dishes, star anise is available in Chinese markets, spice shops, and in some Mexican markets where it is known as *aniz estrella*.

Tofu The Japanese name for bean curd, tofu—a highly nutritious product made from soybeans—has been made in east Asia for over 2,000 years and is an important source of protein for millions of people. As both Asian foods and vegetarian diets grow in popularity in this country, tofu, available in many forms, is becoming a common supermarket item.

In recipes a "cake" of tofu means half a standard package, or about 7 ounces drained weight. Regular, or Japanese-style, tofu is sold packed in liquid in sealed plastic tubs. Because it is fairly fragile, it is best in soups and simmered dishes. Firm, or Chi-

nese-style tofu, is packed similarly to the Japanese kind, but is more compressed. It holds up better in stir-fried dishes and can even be grilled. Both types are also sold in sealed foil packages that do not require refrigeration, but any leftovers must be refrigerated after opening.

Triangles or blocks of fried tofu are used as snacks, stuffed with other ingredients, or cut up in stir-fry dishes. Dried tofu, available in sheets or sticks, is used as a meat substitute in some vegetarian dishes, such as meatless Mu Shu (see page 45).

Vinegars For most Chinese cooking, use a mild, pale vinegar—Japanese rice vinegar is ideal. Be sure to get the unseasoned variety; some types are flavored with salt, sugar, and MSG. Cider vinegar is an approximate substitute for rice vinegar.

A few recipes call for Chinese black vinegar, a dark brown, richly flavored vinegar made from rice wine in Zhejiang province, the same region that produces Shaoxing wine. (Some bottles are labeled "Chekiang" or "Chinkiang," two older spellings of the province.) Italian balsamic vinegar is a close substitute.

Water Chestnuts Canned water chestnuts, like bamboo shoots, vary in quality from one brand to another, so it's a good idea to try different brands. The best ones are sweet and crunchy and have not picked up a metallic taste from the can. They are also available fresh (page 31). Store leftovers covered with water in the refrigerator, changing water daily.

Fresh Chinese-style vegetables like those shown here and described on the opposite page are available increasingly in markets throughout North America.

FRESH INGREDIENTS

An assortment of fresh Chinese-style vegetables are featured in the photograph on the opposite page; clockwise from top: Chinese cabbage, baby bok choy, bitter melon, chiles, coriander (cilantro), long beans, Chinese broccoli, water chestnuts, bean sprouts, turnips, ginger, green onions, watercress, fuzzy melon, and cucumber; in the center are bok choy and bamboo shoots.

Your Chinese dishes will taste best with the freshest ingredients. Whenever possible, shop for vegetables, meats, poultry, and seafood on the day that they will be cooked.

VEGETABLES

Chinese cooking, especially southern style, uses a wide assortment of fresh vegetables. Many of them are becoming available in this country, either imported or home grown to serve the Chinese market. More and more, they are showing up in supermarkets and on produce stands, especially where there is an Asian population. The most common are described below.

Bamboo Shoots Fresh whole bamboo shoots are available in Chinese markets. You should find them stored in cool water to keep them fresh. If stored similarly in cold water in the refrigerator, they will last several days; change the water daily.

Bean Sprouts Sprouted mung beans give a pleasant crunchy texture to many Chinese dishes. (Some stores also carry soybean sprouts, which have larger seeds and require longer cooking.) Look for crisp, white sprouts with a fresh smell; avoid those with withered tails. Buy sprouts the same day you will use them, if possible; otherwise blanch them briefly in boiling water, rinse under cold water, and store in cold water in the refrigerator. Sprouts are easy to grow at home, and most health-food stores sell the beans and specially designed sprouting jars with instructions for their use.

Bitter Melon A member of the gourd family, which includes melons, cucumbers, and squashes, this vegetable looks like a large, wrinkled cucumber. It is typically steamed or blanched to reduce its bitterness, then may be stuffed or used in stir-fried dishes or soups.

Celery Cabbage See Chinese Cabbage.

Chinese Beans Also known as "long beans" or "yard-long beans," these vegetables with elongated pods (actually only about 1½ feet in length) are a little firmer and crunchier than regular green beans, making them excellent for stir-frying. They are available in two colors: a pale and a deeper green. Look for slender, smooth pods without enlarged seeds.

Chinese Cabbage This term covers several members of the cabbage family grown in Asia. One common variety, known in Western markets as "Napa" or "celery cabbage," has tight, cylindrical pale green heads and a mild flavor. The other major type, called *bok choy, pak choy,* or *pak choi,* has loose heads of deep green leaves with contrasting thick white stems. It is slightly stonger in flavor than the celery type. Some markets carry a smaller relative of bok choy; it has greenish stems and is known appropriately enough as "baby bok choy." Recipes will specify which type is to be used.

Coriander, Fresh (Chinese parsley, cilantro) This herb is an essential ingredient in many authentic Chinese recipes. It looks a little like parsley, but the flavor is entirely different. It is a flavor that inspires extreme reactions: Those who like it cannot get enough of it, and others cannot even stand its smell. There is no substitute; if you don't like it or it is unavailable, just leave it out. Ordinary parsley is definitely not a substitute, nor is coriander seed. Fortunately fresh coriander is now widely available in North America, generally under the Spanish name cilantro. Stored with the roots in water and the tops enclosed loosely in a plastic bag, fresh coriander will keep for close to a week.

Fuzzy Melon Another member of the gourd family, fuzzy melon has a slightly hairy green skin and white flesh that tastes a little like cucumber but has a softer texture. Cucumber can be used as a substitute.

Ginger One of the essential flavors of Chinese cuisines, fresh ginger can be sliced, minced, or grated, and it gives a refreshingly clean, hot flavor to all kinds of foods. Most Chinese would not think of cooking seafood without it, and it is equally important to meat and vegetable dishes. Dried, ground ginger (the spice) is not a substitute; fortunately, fresh ginger rhizomes, or so-called ginger roots, are now widely available. Look for rock-hard rhizomes that snap into pieces easily. Fresh ginger will keep for a week or more in the crisper section of the refrigerator. For longer storage, wrap in a paper towel and store in a plastic bag. To prevent mold, change the paper because it absorbs moisture from the ginger.

Green onions Also called "scallions," "spring onions," and even "shallots" in some parts of the country, these slender, young vegetables are widely used in Chinese cooking. Unless otherwise specified in a recipe, use both the white bottoms and the green tops.

Water Chestnuts Chinese markets sometimes sell fresh water chestnuts. The fresh ones are sweeter, crunchier, and altogether preferable to the canned variety (see page 29). Look for rock-hard specimens, and reject any with soft spots.

For the best results in Chinese cooking, seek out the best and freshest meats, poultry, and seafood available in your area.

MEATS AND POULTRY

Although the quantity of meat in the Chinese diet is considerably less than that in the industrial countries of the West, Chinese cooks are notoriously fussy about the quality of meats they will use. Freshness and flavor are valued over all. A Chinese cook will pass by three or four butcher shops on the way to the one that has the freshest pork and will gladly pay more for a freshly killed chicken than for a frozen or packaged bird. Whether you buy from specialty butchers and poulterers or from a supermarket meat case, it pays to shop around and find the very best your neighborhood has to offer.

Pork This is by far the most commonly used meat in Chinese cooking, except among Moslems. The reason is partly economic; pigs can be raised without using scarce space for pasture, and they are an efficient way to convert table and garden scraps into meat. A pig in the backyard has always been so much a part of the rural scene that the Chinese character for "home" combines the characters for "roof" and "pig."

Pork is ideal for Chinese cooking because of its tenderness and relatively mild flavor. It is also surprisingly lean. In fact, well-trimmed pork is leaner than beef; it is not marbled with fat. The loin and rib sections provide the best cuts for stir-frying; for braising, try using spareribs or shoulder cuts.

Beef Although quite popular in Chinese restaurants here, beef is not used to a great extent in China. In most agricultural areas, land is too precious to be used for pasture, and cattle are more valuable as work animals than as a source of meat. The Chinese farmer's cow is seen as a loyal companion and helper, like a cowboy's horse. Furthermore—or perhaps for all these reasons—the Chinese traditionally do not like the taste of beef; they find it too strong.

In adapting to the relative abundance in North America, many Chinese have made beef a regular part of their meals. And in response to Western tastes, dishes such as Broccoli Beef and Oyster Sauce Beef are firmly established on restaurant menus. The best cuts of beef for stir-frying are those that balance tenderness and flavor—round, sirloin, and flatiron, a tender piece within the chuck. Since most stir-fried dishes call for thin slices cut across the grain, even somewhat tougher cuts, such as flank steak, are good choices.

Lamb The Chinese use the same word to cover lamb, mutton, and goat. All of these are used mainly in the arid northwest and by Moslems in other parts of China. Other Chinese consider the flavor of the meat too strong, and it is mainly associated with Mongolian-style grilled or simmered dishes. For moist cooking, use the shoulder; for dry cooking use cuts from the leg or loin.

Chicken A chicken on the table creates a feeling of celebration, or at least of a comfortable family get-together. Chicken is an important part of the Chinese diet, although somewhat less so than pork. All parts of the chicken are savored. Breast meat may be best for stir frying, but the legs, wings, backs, giblets, and even feet give their rich flavor to braised dishes and the chicken stock that is the basis of most Chinese soups. To cook as the Chinese do, go out of your way to find a supplier of good, tasty, fresh chickens. Kosher or Chinese butchers are likely sources.

Duck A much more common meat in China than in this country, duck contains less meat and more fat than a chicken of similar size, but the meat is tastier. Fresh ducks are available increasingly in specialty poultry shops in this country (although you might have to order them ahead of time), and most supermarkets stock or can easily obtain frozen ducks. Incidentally, most domestic ducks in this country—whether from Long Island, New York or Petaluma, California or anywhere in between—are White Pekins, domesticated in China at least as early as the Tang dynasty (A.D. 618-907) and introduced to this country in the nineteenth century.

Other Poultry Birds traditionally used in Chinese cooking include pigeon (squab), pheasant, and quail, as well as wild ducks and geese. Specialty shops in many cities now carry domesticated game birds on a seasonal or special-order basis.

FISH AND SHELLFISH

Products of the sea and of freshwater lakes and rivers have always been an essential part of the Chinese diet. The Chinese were the first to practice aquaculture (fish farming) and have been raising carp and other freshwater fish in ponds for some 2,500 years. To this day a whole fish, a symbol of plenty, is the traditional end to a Chinese banquet.

As with poultry and meats, Chinese cooks are fanatical about freshness in seafood. Whenever possible, they buy a live fish and kill it only minutes before cooking. In Hong Kong's famous seafood restaurants, fish, crabs, and lobsters are kept alive in tanks, and your choice is brought to the table, wriggling and flipping its tail, for approval before being whisked away to the kitchen for cooking.

Fish Most Chinese recipes, such as the steamed fish recipes beginning on page 79, call for a firm, white-fleshed fish that is not too oily. You might try the following saltwater fish: East Coast sea bass, striped bass, tilefish, and cod; Gulf Coast red snapper and smaller grouper or redfish; and West Coast rockfish (also known as rock cod or Pacific snapper). Good choices among freshwater fish are catfish, carp, bass, and pike. For steaming or frying, a whole fish, of 2 to 5 pounds, is ideal. Fillets and steaks of larger fish can also be used. Stronger, richer fish such as salmon, pompano, tuna, or mackerel have more limited use in Chinese cooking, but may be steamed or smoked.

If possible, buy seafood from a specialty market rather than in pre-wrapped packages. Look for a shop that does a brisk business (so the stock turns over quickly) and does not smell too fishy—signs of a fish market that takes extra care to carry only the freshest seafood and handle it properly. Whether buying whole fish, steaks, or fillets, choose those that are brightly colored and have a clean, fresh smell. For tips on choosing a whole fish, see Preparing a Whole Fish, page 20.

Shellfish Shrimp (also known as prawns), crab, and lobster are among the favorite shellfish of Chinese cooks. Whole shrimp are typically stir-fried or deep-fried, and minced or ground shrimp meat finds its way into stuffings for other foods, especially in dim sum. Scallops are used in a number of dishes. Crab and lobster are generally steamed alive, but may be killed and cut up before being stir-fried. Clams are popular in southern Chinese cooking and are typically steamed open before being cooked in a sauce. Squid (calamari) is an excellent feature in stir-fried dishes, and the Chinese have a unique way of preparing it (see Squid with Black Bean Sauce, page 46). Abalone, either fresh or in cans from Australia, is used in soups and stir-fried dishes. A less-expensive alternative to real abalone is a large sea snail from South American waters, available in cans labeled "abalone-type shellfish." Conch and whelk can also be used.

Although Chinese cooks generally avoid it, frozen seafood is acceptable as long as it is recently thawed. Shrimp, squid, abalone, and scallops freeze particularly well. To get them at their freshest, look for those that are still slightly frozen.

Shrimp have more flavor when cooked in the shell rather than peeled. When a recipe calls for cooked and peeled shrimp, as in Cold Noodles With Assorted Toppings (see page 109), devein them with the shells attached, as shown on page 21, place in a bowl with a little minced ginger and a tablespoon or two of Shaoxing wine, and steam in the bowl until meat is opaque white.

CONDIMENTS, SEASONINGS, AND SAUCES

Although the selection of canned goods in a Chinese grocery might seem overwhelming, Chinese cooking actually uses relatively few condiments and prepared sauces. Some of these are easy to make at home.

CHILE OIL

Use this hot, fragrant oil in small quantities whenever you want to add a little chile flavor to sauces, stir-fried, or noodle dishes.

> ½ cup peanut or other
> vegetable oil
> 3 small dried red chiles
> ¼ cup sesame oil

1. Combine peanut oil and chiles in a small saucepan. Heat just until chiles sizzle but do not blacken. Cook a few minutes until fragrant.

2. Turn off heat and add sesame oil. Let oil cool, then transfer to a small jar. To store, cover and keep in a cool, dark place.

Makes ¾ cup.

SICHUAN PEPPER SALT

This flavored salt is used typically as a dry dip for roasted and fried meats and poultry. Try it in place of regular salt in Chinese or Western dishes. The ratio of pepper to salt can be varied to taste.

> 2 tablespoons Sichuan
> peppercorns
> ¼ cup coarse kosher salt

1. Combine peppercorns and salt in a small skillet (preferably with a non-stick surface) and place over medium heat. Cook, stirring or shaking pan frequently, until very fragrant, 3 to 5 minutes.

2. Transfer mixture to a blender, spice grinder, food processor, or mortar, and grind to a fine powder. Store in a tightly covered jar.

Makes ¼ cup.

FIVE-SPICE POWDER

To grind this mixture of spices you will need a sturdy spice or coffee grinder, either an electric mill or a hand-cranked type with a slide-out drawer. A blender with a 1-cup jar will also work.

> 1 teaspoon each *fennel seed,
> cloves, and Sichuan
> peppercorns*
> 1 *cinnamon stick (3-in. piece)*
> 2 *pods star anise*

1. In a dry skillet, toast fennel seed, cloves, and Sichuan peppercorns until fragrant; transfer to grinder.

2. Crumble cinnamon stick and break apart star-anise pod and add to grinder. Grind to a fine powder. Store tightly sealed in a spice jar.

PLUM SAUCE I

Make this version of Chinese plum sauce throughout the year using commonly available ingredients. If possible, make at least one day ahead to allow the flavors to ripen.

> 2 *teaspoons cornstarch*
> ½ *cup water*
> ⅓ *cup plum preserves*
> ¼ *cup apricot-pineapple
> preserves*
> 3 *tablespoons rice vinegar*
> 2 *cloves garlic, minced*
> 1 *teaspoon minced ginger*
> ½ *teaspoon kosher salt*
> 1 *small dried chile, seeded and
> roughly chopped or ½ tea-
> spoon dried chile flakes*

1. In a small saucepan, dissolve cornstarch in water. Add preserves and vinegar.

2. Combine garlic, ginger, and salt in a mortar and pound to a paste. *Or:* Combine on cutting board and mash repeatedly with the side of a wide-bladed French or Chinese knife. Add paste and chopped chile to sauce.

3. Bring sauce to a boil and reduce to a simmer. Cook until slightly thickened. To test, spoon a little sauce onto a cool plate. It should hold its shape or run just slightly. If too thin, reduce further. Serve at room temperature; store in refrigerator.

Makes ¾ cup.

PLUM SAUCE II

When fresh plums are in season, try canning a year-round supply of plum sauce. The flavor of this sauce will improve with a month of storage.

> 2 *pounds ripe red or yellow
> plums, sliced*
> 2 *pounds ripe apricots or
> peaches, sliced*
> 2 *red bell peppers, quartered,
> seeds and ribs removed*
> 2½ *cups rice or cider vinegar*
> 2 *cups water*
> 2 *cups sugar*
> ⅓ *cup light corn syrup*
> 2 *tablespoons minced garlic*
> ¼ *cup minced ginger*
> 1½ *tablespoons kosher salt*
> 3 *small dried chiles, seeded and
> roughly chopped*

1. In a large noncorrodible saucepan or stockpot, simmer plums, apricots, and peppers in vinegar and 1 cup water until tender (about 20 minutes).

2. Dissolve sugar and corn syrup in remaining water and add to pot. Add garlic, ginger, salt, and chiles. Simmer 1 hour, stirring occasionally.

3. Purée mixture through medium disk of a food mill to remove skins. Return to pot and bring to a boil. Continue to boil gently until sauce thickens (10 to 15 minutes), stirring frequently.

4. Ladle hot sauce into washed and heated pint or half-pint jars, leaving 1- to 2-inch headspace; seal. Process in boiling-water bath for 10 minutes.

Makes 4 pints.

MAKE-AHEAD SAUCES

Stir-frying and many other Chinese cooking techniques are a quick form of cooking, but they do require a certain amount of time for assembling and cutting the ingredients. However, the preparation time can be reduced by using one of the bottled stir-fry sauces now showing up in many grocery stores or by making your own sauce ahead of time and storing it in the refrigerator. With these sauces, a stir-fry dish such as Cantonese Red-Pepper Chicken (see page 42) can be assembled, cooked, and served in less than 15 minutes.

Caution The following recipes are not designed for home canning. The sauces are too low in acid to safely store at room temperature. However, if stored tightly covered in the refrigerator, they should keep for a week or more, making them ideal to prepare ahead of time and use for quick weeknight meals.

BLACK BEAN SAUCE

Use this sauce by itself over steamed fish or as a component in stir-fried or braised dishes.

- ¼ cup fermented black beans (see page 26), roughly chopped
- 2 to 3 tablespoons Shaoxing wine or dry sherry
- ¼ cup Basic Chicken Stock (see page 64)
- 2 tablespoons dark soy sauce
- 1 teaspoon cornstarch
- 1 tablespoon oil
- 2 tablespoons minced ginger
- 1 tablespoon minced garlic

1. In a small bowl combine black beans and wine to cover. Set aside to soak 15 minutes. In another bowl combine stock, soy sauce, and cornstarch.

2. In a small skillet or saucepan, heat oil over low heat. Add ginger and garlic and cook slowly, stirring occasionally, until fragrant but not browned. Add beans and wine and bring to a boil. Stir stock mixture to dissolve cornstarch and add to pan. Simmer sauce until thickened, and transfer to a clean glass jar. Store in refrigerator. Sauce will keep for a week or more.

Makes about ½ cup.

Timesaver sauces: Plum Sauce I, left; Black Bean Sauce, top right; and Sichuan Hot Bean Sauce can all be made up to a week ahead of time and used in a variety of dishes.

SICHUAN HOT BEAN SAUCE

This sauce features a typically Sichuan-style blend of flavors—hot, sour, salty, and sweet. Use it as an instant stir-fry sauce for chicken, shredded pork or beef, or cubes of firm tofu; or stir it into a bowl of noodles moistened with stock.

- ⅓ cup water or Basic Chicken Stock (see page 64)
- 4 teaspoons black vinegar
- 1 to 1½ teaspoons brown sugar
- 1 tablespoon oil
- 2 tablespoons each minced ginger and garlic
- ¼ cup minced green onion
- 1 teaspoon red pepper flakes
- ⅓ cup canned brown bean sauce or miso
  Chile oil, to taste

1. Combine water, vinegar, and brown sugar and stir to dissolve sugar. In a small skillet or saucepan, heat oil over low heat. Add ginger, garlic, green onion, and pepper flakes and cook, stirring frequently, until fragrant but not browned.

2. Add bean sauce and vinegar mixture, bring to a boil, and cook until slightly reduced. Taste sauce for balance (it will be quite salty, but hot, sour, and sweet flavors should be noticeable); adjust as necessary with more vinegar, sugar, or chile oil.

3. Transfer to a clean glass jar and refrigerate until ready to use. Sauce will keep for a week or more.

Makes about ½ cup.

TABLE SAUCES

Most Chinese dishes are finished in the kitchen and are not further seasoned at the table. A few foods, such as dim sum, steamed vegetables, and simple steamed or simmered chicken, may be served with dipping sauces.

SWEET AND SOUR DIPPING SAUCE

Sweet and sour sauces taste good with fried appetizers, especially if they are not too sweet. Try this sauce with Phoenix Tail Fried Shrimp (page 52) or Shanghai Spring Rolls (page 122).

- ½ cup water
- ¼ cup rice vinegar
- 3 tablespoons brown sugar
- 1 teaspoon tomato paste
- 1 tablespoon minced ginger
- 1 clove garlic, minced
- 1 teaspoon soy sauce
- 1 teaspoon cornstarch

1. In a small saucepan, combine ¼ cup water, vinegar, sugar, tomato paste, ginger, garlic, and soy sauce and bring to a boil. Reduce heat and simmer 5 minutes.

2. Dissolve cornstarch in remaining water and add to sauce. Simmer until glossy. Strain before serving.

Makes ⅔ cup.

HOT MUSTARD SAUCE

Unlike Western mustards, the typical Chinese mustard sauce is a simple paste of dry mustard and water. Use it in small quantities, mixed with soy sauce or perhaps sweet-and-sour sauce. Here, vinegar and sesame oil provide a smooth flavor.

- 3 tablespoons warm water
- 1 tablespoon rice vinegar
- ¼ cup dry mustard
- 1 teaspoon sesame oil

Combine water and vinegar and stir in mustard. Blend until smooth and stir in sesame oil. Let stand at least 30 minutes before serving, preferably longer. Can be stored in a tightly covered jar.

Makes ½ cup.

SOY-BASED DIPPING SAUCES

Soy sauce with a little something mixed in provides an endless variety of dipping sauces. Each recipe makes an individual serving.

Soy and Chile Oil Dipping Sauce 1 tablespoon soy, ½ teaspoon chile oil (or to taste). Use for steamed dumplings.

Soy-Ginger Dipping Sauce 1 tablespoon soy sauce, ½ teaspoon grated or finely minced ginger, a few drops sesame oil. For poached or steamed chicken.

Shellfish Dipping Sauce 1 tablespoon soy sauce, 1 teaspoon grated ginger, ½ teaspoon rice vinegar. Especially good with crab or shrimp.

Soy and Mustard Dipping Sauce 1 tablespoon soy sauce, Hot Mustard Sauce (at left) or Dijon-style mustard to taste. For dumplings or vegetables with pork stuffings.

DUCK SAUCES

A thick, slightly sweet sauce based on hoisin or, less commonly, plum sauce is a traditional accompaniment to roast duck and is equally good with Mu Shu Pork (see page 45). Simply combine the listed ingredients and serve in small bowls for diners to use as desired.

Duck Sauce I

- 4 tablespoons canned Chinese or homemade plum sauce (Plum Sauce I or II, page 34)
- 1 tablespoon regular or dark soy sauce
- ½ teaspoon sesame oil

Duck Sauce II

- 4 tablespoons hoisin sauce
- ½ teaspoon black soy sauce
- ½ teaspoon sesame oil
  Pinch of sugar

Duck Sauce III

- 1 tablespoon brown bean sauce
- 3 tablespoons plum preserves
- ½ teaspoon each rice vinegar and water
- ½ teaspoon sesame oil

Anzen Importers
736 NE Union Avenue
Portland, OR 97232
(503) 233-5111
Chinese, Japanese, and other Asian food, cookware, vegetable seeds; telephone orders accepted.

Oriental Food Market and Cooking School
2801 West Howard
Chicago, IL 60645
(312) 274-2826
Foods, cookware, books; direct orders to Pansy or Chu-yen Luke.

Woks 'n' Things
2234 South Wentworth Avenue
Chicago, IL 60616
(312) 842-0701
Cookware and supplies only; telephone orders accepted; no charge for catalog; direct orders to Ken Moy.

The Oriental Market
502 Pampas Street
Austin, TX 78752
(512) 453-9058

Oriental Food Mart
909 Race Street
Philadelphia, PA 19107
(215) 922-5111

Soya Food Products
2356 Wyoming Avenue
Cincinnati, OH 45214
(513) 661-2250
Tofu manufacturer, other foods, cookware; send SASE for catalog; telephone orders accepted.

Uwajimaya, Inc.
519 Sixth Avenue South
Seattle, WA 98104
(206) 624-6248
Mostly Japanese products, but many Chinese ones, too; telephone orders accepted.

Wing Woh Lung Co.
50 Mott Street
New York, NY 10013
(212) 962-3459
Telephone orders accepted.

Wing Fat Co., Inc.
35 Mott Street
New York, NY 10013
(212) 962-0433

Special Feature

WHERE TO SHOP FOR CHINESE GOODS

As the interest in Chinese and other Asian cooking continues to grow, more and more supermarkets are stocking Asian-style vegetables, soy sauce and other condiments, dried mushrooms, noodles, and dough wrappers. Most well-stocked cookware stores carry woks and their basic accessories. For the less common ingredients and equipment, you will probably need to find a Chinese market. Wherever there is an Asian community, which means most large cities in the United States, there are bound to be some stores carrying Chinese foods and cookware. Check the yellow pages under Asian (or Oriental) Goods. Fortunately, most Chinese canned and dried goods have a long shelf life, so you can stock up for several months' worth of cooking on a single trip.

One possible source of Chinese-style produce is your own garden. Nurseries and seed catalogs carry seeds for many Asian vegetables, including bok choy and other cabbages, coriander, Chinese beans, Asian eggplants, bitter melon, and fuzzy melon. All these vegetables can be grown wherever their Western counterparts will grow.

If there is no Asian market in your area, try one of the following mail-order sources for non-perishable foods and other supplies. Except as noted, all sell foods and cookware. Most can provide a catalog or price list, and some take telephone orders as well.

*The ancient and versatile wok
can be used to prepare all kinds
of Chinese dishes. Stir-frying
and deep-frying are two popular
wok cooking techniques.*

Stir-Frying & Deep-Frying

Chinese cooking methods can be broken down into three main categories: cooking with oil, cooking with water, and cooking with dry heat. We begin with two techniques of cooking in oil—the uniquely Chinese stir-frying method and the cosmopolitan technique of deep-frying. In China these are more typical of restaurant cooking than of cooking done at home, but they are easy techniques that can be mastered by any cook.

STIR-FRYING

Although they sound quite similar, stir-frying, pan-frying, and deep-frying are actually three distinct cooking techniques involving different amounts of oil. Pan-frying—cooking large pieces in a flat-bottomed pan with a shallow layer of oil—is not common in Chinese cooking, except for a few items (see Ginger Beef Chow Fun, page 108). Stir-frying and frying in deep oil, on the other hand, are widely used cooking techniques that usually account for more than half of the items on a Chinese restaurant menu.

Stir-frying is the most typically Chinese cooking technique. Stir-frying means cooking bite-sized pieces of meats and vegetables quickly over high heat in a small amount of oil. The food is cooked by both the heat of the pan and the heat carried by the oil. As the name implies, the ingredients are stirred almost constantly during cooking so that they cook evenly. It is an ideal way to preserve colors, flavors, textures, and nutritional value of foods.

Cooking fuel has traditionally been scarce in China, and Chinese cooks have always sought ways of cooking foods with a minimum of fuel. Stir-frying is a perfect example; cutting up the ingredients into small pieces increases the surface area, decreasing the cooking time. In the traditional Chinese kitchen, the heat source was a charcoal fire in a small clay brazier. The fire was fanned until it glowed red-hot, and then food was quickly cooked before the heat could die down.

In a modern kitchen, where the cooking heat can be controlled with the twist of a knob, the principles of stir-frying remain the same. For busy modern cooks, time is the most precious commodity, and stir-frying is one of the best ways to produce delicious dishes in a short time.

A wok is the ideal pan for stir-frying, but the following recipes can also be prepared in a large skillet or even an electric skillet. Bear in mind, however, that a flat-bottomed skillet will require more oil to keep the food from sticking.

Because everything happens quickly in stir-frying, organization is essential. Once you start cooking a stir-fried dish, there is no time to cut up the ginger or carrots or to run to the kitchen cabinet for the oyster sauce. So cut, measure, marinate, and assemble all the ingredients before you turn on the heat.

PREPARATION PLAN

Although the details vary, the same techniques apply to all stir-fried dishes. The following list explains the steps in preparing a typical stir-fried dish, Cantonese Red-Pepper Chicken.

☐ *Marinate.* If any ingredients need marinating or soaking, this should be done first. In this dish, the chicken cubes are marinated in a mixture of soy sauce and wine, which both flavors the meat and tenderizes it slightly. Some other marinades include egg white or cornstarch, which add a slight coating to seal in the flavor and juices during cooking. If a recipe includes dried mushrooms, salted black beans, or any other ingredient that must be soaked before cooking, this is the time to do it. (In this dish, however, the beans are not soaked before cooking.)

☐ *Cut up.* While the chicken is marinating, peel, slice, mince, and dice the remaining ingredients to the required sizes and shapes. This can be done hours ahead of time and the ingredients wrapped and refrigerated.

☐ *Assemble.* To save time and counter space, try to combine ingredients that will go into the wok at the same time. In this case, the ginger, garlic, green onions, and chiles can be combined in one bowl, and the cornstarch can be dissolved in water in another. Don't mix liquid and dry ingredients unless you are specifically directed to do so. This is also the time to assemble all the tools you will need—oil can, spatula, cooking chopsticks, wire skimmer (for straining the chicken out of its marinade), and ladle (for serving)—and the serving plate. If you will have to keep the dish hot for any length of time before serving, turn the oven on a low setting to warm the plate and hold the finished dish until ready.

☐ *Heat wok and add oil.* For best results, heat the wok first, then add the oil in a thin stream around the outside of the pan. As the oil slides down the hot sides, it both heats to the perfect cooking temperature and oils the sides of the wok to keep the food from sticking. If you accidentally pour in too much oil, do not try to pour it out of the wok; instead, swab the excess out with a paper towel and discard.

☐ *Stir-fry meat.* By the time most of the oil has run down into the middle of the wok, it is ready for the chicken; wait much longer and the oil will burn. Scatter the chicken cubes over the bottom of the pan and immediately begin stirring and tossing with the spatula. As you stir, move the more-cooked pieces out of the center and the outside pieces will fall in to take their places. Some recipes, including the following one, call for cooking the meat first and then removing it while the vegetables cook. In others, the ingredients are simply added to the pan according to their relative cooking time so that they all finish at once. Each recipe will specify the technique to use.

☐ *Stir-fry vegetables.* Aromatic ingredients, such as ginger, garlic, and green onion, are typically cooked in the oil by themselves, either before or after you cook the meat. This separate cooking flavors the oil, carrying their aroma through the dish. At this stage, do not cook them so long that they brown; cook them only until they are fragrant. They will continue to cook along with the other ingredients.

☐ *Add liquids.* Most stir-fried dishes involve some liquid, but it is not added until after the main ingredients have cooked for a while in oil. Adding the liquids too soon will result in braised foods, with a different texture than that of stir-fried food.

☐ *Thicken.* Cornstarch is the typical thickener for stir-fried dishes, especially those from southern China. It should always be dissolved in cold or room-temperature liquid before being added to a hot sauce. Although it works quickly, allow cornstarch enough time to cook or the sauce will have a raw, "starchy" flavor. When the sauce loses its cloudy appearance and begins to glisten (usually less than a minute), it is done. Not all stir-fried dishes are thickened, and if you prefer, you can leave the cornstarch out of the following recipes without any harm. You might wish to use a little less liquid or reduce the sauce further in that case.

☐ *Taste and serve.* Taste a bite of the dish with chopsticks. Is the balance of seasonings right? If not, adjust it. Is the sauce thickened the right amount, so that it clings to each bite? If not, reduce it a little further. If the sauce is too thin but the dish is otherwise fully cooked, transfer the meat and vegetables to the serving dish and boil the sauce down before pouring it. If your wok has a long handle, it is easy to pour the dish out onto the serving platter, scraping the sauce over it with the spatula. If it does not, scoop the food into the ladle with the spatula and transfer to the serving dish a ladleful at a time. If possible, rinse the wok out immediately with hot water and return it to the heat to dry; otherwise, be sure to wash it as soon as possible.

Use Your Senses

Because of variations in cookware, heat of the stove, and size of ingredients, precise cooking times are difficult to give. Instead, most of the recipes in this chapter give directions like "cook until fragrant," "stir-fry until meat loses its raw color," and so on. Learn to trust your senses and adjust recipe instructions as needed.

These stir-fry recipes are also not precise as to the amount of oil, which is usually given simply as "oil for stir-frying." How much oil you should use depends upon the size and condition of your wok (a well-seasoned wok will require less oil to keep foods from sticking), but 1 to 2 tablespoons should suffice in most cases. If the food sticks or seems to be cooking too dry, add a little more oil around the edge of the pan. It will heat up as it slides down the sides.

CANTONESE RED-PEPPER CHICKEN
South China

This is an adaptation of a Cantonese dish, usually made with dried red-pepper flakes. Here, the fresh chiles add both color and another texture. If fresh red chiles are not available, use a red bell pepper and add ½ teaspoon dried red-pepper flakes with the ginger and garlic.

- 2 whole chicken breasts, boned, skinned, and cut into ½-inch cubes
- 1 tablespoon each *soy sauce and Shaoxing wine or dry sherry*
- 1 tablespoon each *minced ginger and garlic*
- ¼ cup sliced green onions
- 4 fresh red jalapeño chiles, seeded and cut into ½-inch squares
  Oil, for stir-frying
- 2 tablespoons fermented black beans
- ½ cup Basic Chicken Stock (see page 64)
- ½ teaspoon cornstarch dissolved in a little water

1. Combine chicken cubes with soy sauce and wine, and marinate for 30 minutes or longer. Combine ginger, garlic, green onions, and chiles; set aside.

2. Heat wok over medium-high heat, and add oil. Drain chicken and discard marinade. Stir-fry chicken until opaque and springy, about 3 minutes. Remove from pan.

3. Add another 2 tablespoons oil to wok and stir-fry ginger, garlic, green onion, and chiles until fragrant. Add black beans and stock; bring to a boil. Add cornstarch mixture and cook until thickened. Return chicken to wok to reheat briefly, and serve.

Serves 6 to 8 with other dishes.

SOUTHWESTERN CHINA

The mountainous inland provinces of southwestern China, particularly Sichuan and Hunan, are home to some of the tastiest dishes in the Chinese repertoire. It is a region of hot, humid summers and cold winters, of high mountains and deep river gorges. The food also tends toward extremes: Nowhere in China are chile peppers used more liberally. In fact, the climate is one reason for the popularity of chiles; in hot weather, eating chiles induces perspiration, which in turn has a cooling effect. In winter, chile-flavored foods leave a warm glow.

The foods of the southwest have long been popular in other regions of China and in the last few decades have become popular overseas. Chefs from Sichuan and Hunan have opened restaurants in North America and found an eager, chile-loving audience, appetites whetted by Mexican cooking, eager to explore other "chile cuisines."

There is much more to China's southwestern food than hot pepper, however. Sichuanese cooking often combines hot, sour, and salty flavors in one dish. Shredded Eggplant With Minced Pork (page 48) is an example. Twice-cooked pork, *kung pao* dishes, and peanut- and sesame-based sauces are also typical of the robust flavors of Sichuan cooking. Hunanese cuisine is similar, although many dishes are not as hot as their Sichuan counterparts. Duck or other meats smoked over aromatic woods, tea, and spices are popular in both provinces. The dry-cured ham of Yunnan figures in many regional dishes.

Subtropical Yunnan and Guizhou provinces, which border Burma, Laos, and Vietnam, contain many non-Chinese minorities. Not surprisingly, the food shows Southeast Asian and Indian influences. A typical Yunnan curry might combine Thai-style spices with Cantonese-style black beans.

CASHEW VELVET CHICKEN

"Velvet chicken" has two meanings. In one sense, it refers to breast meat that has been minced with a cleaver to a fluffy consistency (see Sizzling Rice Soup, page 66). It also refers to this technique, in which cubes of meat marinated in egg white are given a preliminary cooking in oil before stir-frying.

- 2 tablespoons each *soy sauce and Shaoxing wine or dry sherry*
- 1 egg white
  Pinch of salt
- 1 teaspoon cornstarch
- 1 whole chicken breast, boned and skinned
- ¼ cup Basic Chicken Stock (see page 64)
- ½ cup oil
- ¼ cup raw cashews
- 1 tablespoon minced ginger
- ½ cup sliced celery
- ½ cup diced or sliced bamboo shoots

1. In a medium bowl, combine 1 tablespoon of the soy sauce with wine, egg white, salt, and ½ teaspoon of the cornstarch; blend thoroughly. Cut chicken into ¼-inch cubes and toss in marinade to coat thoroughly. Set aside to marinate for 30 minutes to several hours. Combine stock and remaining soy sauce and cornstarch; set aside.

2. Heat wok over medium heat, and add oil. Add cashews and fry until golden brown. Remove and drain on paper towels.

3. Drain excess marinade from chicken pieces. Fry chicken just until firm, about 45 seconds. Remove and drain on paper towels.

4. Remove all but 2 tablespoons oil from wok. Increase heat to medium-high. Add ginger and stir-fry until fragrant. Add celery and bamboo shoots. Stir-fry 1 minute; add chicken and cashews and cook until chicken is done, about 2 minutes more. Stir stock to dissolve cornstarch, and add to pan. Cook over high heat until sauce thickens, and serve.

Serves 4 to 6 with other dishes.

CHICKEN WITH ALMONDS AND HAM

This approach to stir-fried chicken, without the initial "velveting" step, is simpler than that used in Cashew Velvet Chicken. The meat has a firmer texture this way; see which one you prefer. All stir-fried chicken dishes can be prepared with either technique, "velveted" or not.

- 1 whole chicken breast, boned and cut into ⅜-inch cubes
- 1 tablespoon each *dark soy sauce and Shaoxing wine or dry sherry*
- ½ teaspoon cornstarch
- 2 tablespoons Basic Chicken Stock (see page 64) or water
- 1 small cucumber
- 3 tablespoons oil
- ¼ cup blanched whole almonds
- 2 tablespoons each *minced ginger and green onion*
- 1 ounce Smithfield ham, soaked and thinly sliced
- 1 red or green bell pepper, seeded and diced

1. Combine chicken cubes with soy sauce and wine, and marinate for 30 minutes. Combine cornstarch and stock; set aside.

2. With a vegetable peeler, remove thin lengthwise strips of cucumber skin ½ inch apart to make a pattern of alternating green and white. Split cucumber lengthwise, remove seeds if desired, and cut across into thick (³⁄₁₆-inch) slices.

3. Heat wok over medium-high heat, and add oil. Add almonds and stir-fry until lightly browned. Remove and drain on paper towels.

4. Drain chicken and add any remaining marinade to stock mixture. Remove all but 1 tablespoon oil from wok and increase heat to high. Add ginger and green onion; cook until fragrant. Add chicken and stir-fry just until it begins to lose its raw color. Add ham, cucumber slices, peppers, and almonds. Stir-fry until chicken is done, then add stock mixture. Bring to a boil and cook until the sauce thickens.

Serves 4 to 6 with other dishes.

KUNG PAO CHICKEN
Southwestern China

Kung pao dishes are among the most popular items in Sichuan-style restaurants everywhere. Their characteristic flavor comes from charring dried chiles in the oil before stir-frying the main ingredient. Unfortunately, this tends to produce an acrid smoke that can irritate the cook's nose and eyes, so use your stove's hood fan if it has one. If not, stop cooking the chiles a little short of the charring point; the dish will still be delicious.

> 2 tablespoons each *soy sauce and Shaoxing wine or dry sherry*
> 1 *egg white*
>   *Pinch of salt*
> 1 *teaspoon cornstarch*
> 1 *whole chicken breast, boned, skinned, and cut into ⅜-inch cubes*
> ¼ cup *Basic Chicken Stock (see page 64)*
> ½ cup *oil*
> ¼ cup *shelled raw peanuts*
> 2 or 3 *small dried chiles*
> 2 tablespoons each *minced ginger and garlic*
>   *Pinch of red-pepper flakes*
> 2 or 3 *green onions, cut into 1-inch lengths*
> ½ cup *seeded and diced red bell peppers or fresh red chiles*
> ¼ cup *diced bamboo shoots*

1. In a medium bowl, combine 1 tablespoon of the soy sauce with wine, egg white, salt, and ½ teaspoon of the cornstarch; blend thoroughly. Toss chicken in marinade to coat thoroughly. Set aside to marinate for 30 minutes to several hours. Combine the stock and remaining soy sauce and cornstarch; set aside.

2. Heat wok over medium-high heat, and add oil. Add peanuts and fry until golden brown. Remove and drain on paper towels.

3. Drain excess marinade from the chicken pieces. Fry chicken, half at a time, just until firm, about 45 seconds. Remove and drain on paper towels.

4. Remove all but 2 tablespoons oil from pan (oil may be strained and reserved for another use). Add dried chiles to wok and stir-fry over medium-high heat until nearly blackened; remove. Add ginger, garlic, and red-pepper flakes; stir-fry until fragrant. Add green onions, peppers, and bamboo shoots; stir-fry 1 minute. Add chicken and peanuts and cook until chicken is done, about 2 minutes more. Stir stock to dissolve cornstarch, and add to pan. Cook over high heat until sauce thickens, and serve immediately.

Serves 4 to 6 with other dishes.

Tender chicken, crunchy peanuts and vegetables, and dried chiles seared in hot oil are combined in this pungent southwestern-style Kung Pao Chicken.

Stir-frying is an ideal way to preserve the flavor and crunchy texture of fresh asparagus. Here Beef With Asparagus makes for a springtime treat.

BEEF WITH ASPARAGUS

When asparagus is in season, virtually every Chinese restaurant features this simple but delicious stir-fry.

    2   teaspoons minced ginger
    2   tablespoons Shaoxing wine
        or dry sherry
    3   tablespoons dark soy sauce or
        2 parts light and 1 part black
        soy sauce
    ½   teaspoon sesame oil
    ½   pound lean beef, sliced into
        stir-frying strips
    1½ teaspoons cornstarch
    2 to 3 tablespoons oil
    1   pound asparagus, roll cut
        into 2-inch pieces

1. In a medium bowl, combine ginger, wine, soy sauce, and sesame oil. Toss the beef strips in mixture, and marinate for 30 minutes to several hours.

2. Drain beef well and reserve marinade. Combine marinade with enough water to make ⅓ cup. Dissolve cornstarch in this mixture.

3. Heat wok over high heat, and add 1 tablespoon of the oil. Add beef to pan; stir-fry until meat loses its raw color, about 1 minute. Remove meat from pan.

4. Add remaining oil to wok. Add asparagus and stir-fry over medium heat until just heated through. Return beef to pan; add reserved marinade. Increase heat to high and cook until sauce thickens. Serve immediately.

Serves 4 to 6 with other dishes.

Variation When asparagus is not in season, sliced Chinese or Western-style broccoli can be used in its place. Blanch, if desired (see Broccoli With Black Bean Sauce, page 50).

Variation For a richer sauce, reduce soy sauce in marinade to 1 tablespoon dark soy; add 2 tablespoons oyster sauce to pan in step 4.

MU SHU PORK
Northern China

This Beijing-style dish is one of the most popular selections in Mandarin restaurants in this country. Part of the reason is that it is fun to eat. Beef, chicken, pork, or dark-meat turkey can also be prepared *mu shu* style. A photograph of this dish appears on page 17.

    3   green onions
    1   tablespoon grated ginger
    1   tablespoon soy sauce
    2   tablespoons water or
        half water and half
        Shaoxing wine
        Pinch of sugar
    3   tablespoons oil
    2   eggs, lightly beaten
    ½   pound lean pork, in
        matchstick shreds
    ¼   cup shredded bamboo shoots
    ¼   cup each lily buds and cloud
        ears, soaked in warm water
        and drained
    8   warm Mandarin Pancakes
        (see page 114)
    ¼   cup Duck Sauce (see page 36)
        or hoisin sauce

1. Separate green onions into green tops and white bases. Cut white parts into shreds and combine with ginger. Cut green tops into shreds and set aside. Combine soy sauce, water, and sugar; set aside.

2. Heat wok over medium heat. Add 1 tablespoon of the oil and swirl to coat sides of pan. Add eggs and cook just until set. Remove eggs to cutting board, and cut into thin strips.

3. Wipe wok clean and return to heat. Add remaining oil, and, when hot, add ginger–green onion mixture. Stir-fry until fragrant, and add pork. Cook just until pork loses its raw color. Add bamboo shoots, lily buds, and cloud ears; stir-fry 2 minutes longer. Add soy sauce mixture and egg strips, increase heat to high, and cook until nearly all liquid is evaporated. Taste for seasoning, and transfer to serving platter.

4. Serve warm Mandarin Pancakes on a separate plate, with green-onion shreds and Duck Sauce in small dishes. For each serving, spread a pancake with ½ teaspoon or so of the sauce, add a few green onion shreds, and top with some of the pork mixture. Roll the pancake around the filling and eat with the fingers.

Serves 4 to 6 with other dishes.

Variation For a delicious vegetarian version of Mu Shu Pork, substitute 1 package fried tofu (see page 29), shredded, for the pork. Add ¼ cup shredded carrots and 2 black mushroom caps, minced, along with the bamboo shoots in step 3.

BLACK-PEPPER BEEF

Our familiar black pepper is a foreign spice in China, but that has not stopped Chinese chefs from incorporating it into their cuisine.

    ¾   pound lean, tender beef,
        thinly sliced
    2   tablespoons dark soy sauce
    ½   teaspoon coarsely ground
        black pepper
    ½   cup Basic Chicken Stock
        (see page 64)
        Oil, for stir-frying
    1   tablespoon minced ginger
    4   green onions, cut into
        1-inch pieces
    1   teaspoon sesame oil

1. Combine beef slices with 1 tablespoon of the soy sauce and the pepper, and marinate for 30 minutes. Drain beef, reserving marinade. Combine marinade with stock and remaining soy sauce.

2. Heat wok over high heat, and add oil. Add ginger; cook until fragrant. Add beef and green onions; stir-fry just until beef loses its raw color. Add stock mixture and cook until reduced by half. Sprinkle sesame oil over all, and serve.

Serves 4 to 6 with other dishes.

Variation Bok choy, Chinese mustard, watercress, or other greens can be included. Remove beef from wok after initial cooking, then add 1 cup sliced greens; stir-fry until wilted. Return beef and green onions to pan, and add liquids.

THE TIGER
Third sign of the zodiac
Magnetic, aggressive, adventuro'
large ego and an unpred'
r. But

A perennial favorite, Shrimp With Snow Peas and Water Chestnuts is even better when made with fresh water chestnuts.

SQUID WITH BLACK BEAN SAUCE
Southern China

Small squid, known as calamari, make an excellent stir-fry. The Chinese have developed an easy way to clean and cut squid that also gives an attractive result. When the diamond-cut squid cooks, it curls into little cylinders shaped like pine cones.

> 1 *pound whole squid, fresh or thawed*
>   *Oil, for stir-frying*
> 1 *tablespoon each minced ginger and garlic*
> ¼ *teaspoon red-pepper flakes*
> 2 *green onions, cut into 1-inch slices*
> ½ *cup red or green bell peppers, seeded and cut into 1-inch squares*
> 2 *tablespoons fermented black beans, soaked for 15 minutes in 2 tablespoons each water and Shaoxing wine or dry sherry*

1. *To clean and cut squid:* With a Chinese knife or a smaller knife, cut just below eyes to cut off tentacles in one piece. Squeeze out and discard beak, a small, hard object in center of tentacles. Slice sac open lengthwise; avoid cutting into ink sac, a small, silvery tube about an inch long. Hold tail end of sac down against board with one hand and scrape away entrails and transparent quill. Discard outer purplish skin, if desired. Holding knife at an angle, cut almost through sac with parallel diagonal cuts about ½ inch apart. Repeat at a 60-degree angle to first set of cuts to make a diamond pattern. Small sacs may be left whole; cut larger sacs into 2 or 3 pieces. Rinse sacs and tentacles, and drain thoroughly.

2. Heat wok over high heat, and add oil. Add ginger, garlic, and pepper flakes; stir-fry until fragrant. Add green onions and peppers; stir-fry until heated through, adjusting heat if necessary so that garlic does not burn. Add squid and stir-fry until pieces begin to curl and stiffen, about 30 seconds. Add black bean mixture and cook 1 minute, stirring to coat ingredients evenly with sauce. Serve immediately.

Serves 4 to 6 with other dishes.

STIR-FRIED CRAB
Eastern China

This tasty Shanghai-style dish is best made from a live crab that you kill and clean yourself (steps 1 and 2, below). However, a precooked or cooked and frozen crab will benefit from the bright, gingery sauce. If you are buying a precooked crab, you might want to have it cleaned and cracked by the fishmonger. If you are using a frozen crab, be sure it is thoroughly thawed. Allow crab to come to room temperature before stir-frying.

- 1 Dungeness crab, about 2 pounds, or 2 pounds blue crabs
  Oil, for stir-frying
- 3 tablespoons finely grated ginger
- 2 tablespoons each soy sauce and Shaoxing wine or dry sherry
- ¼ cup Basic or Rich Chicken Stock (see page 64)
- 2 green onions, cut into 2-inch lengths and shredded
  Shredded green onions or fresh coriander sprigs, for garnish

1. If using a live crab, kill it by plunging it into boiling water for 1 minute. Rinse with cold water to stop cooking. If using a cooked crab, begin with next step.

2. Hold crab by body and lift off top shell. Turn crab over and remove triangular "breastplate" on underside, together with soft spines hidden underneath. Turn top side up again and remove gray, feathery gills. Remove jaws and intestine, a crooked white tube running from front to back. Remaining spongy mass of tissue (olive green in uncooked crab, pale yellow when fully cooked) is mostly fat; discard or reserve for another use. Rinse body of crab until only meat and shell remain.

3. Split body down the middle, then cut each half between legs into 5 pieces, each attached to a leg or claw. Crack each section of leg and claw with one sharp blow of a mallet.

4. Heat wok over medium-high heat, and add oil. When oil is hot enough to sizzle a bit of ginger, add half the crab pieces; stir-fry until shells are bright red and meat is opaque, 3 to 4 minutes. Remove crab to a heated platter; repeat with remaining pieces. Add a little more oil, if necessary, and stir-fry ginger until fragrant. Add soy sauce, wine, and stock; bring to a boil. Add green onions, return crab to pan, and cook 1 minute. Serve garnished with shredded green onions.

Serves 4 with other dishes.

SHRIMP WITH SNOW PEAS AND WATER CHESTNUTS

This is a study in crisp textures and bright, complementary colors. Splitting the shrimp lengthwise causes them to curl into spirals when cooked. It also gives you twice as many pieces!

- ½ pound shrimp, peeled and split lengthwise
  Pinch of salt
- 2 tablespoons Shaoxing wine or dry sherry
  Oil, for stir-frying
- 1 tablespoon minced ginger
- ½ pound snow peas, stems and strings removed
- ½ cup sliced water chestnuts (preferably fresh)
- 1 tablespoon soy sauce
- ½ teaspoon cornstarch dissolved in ¼ cup water or stock

1. Toss shrimp with salt, add wine, and marinate for 20 minutes to several hours.

2. Drain shrimp and reserve marinade. Heat wok over high heat, and add oil. Add ginger, stir-fry until fragrant, and add shrimp. Stir-fry until shrimp are mostly opaque, 2 to 4 minutes, depending on size.

3. Add snow peas and water chestnuts; stir-fry until just heated through. Add reserved marinade, soy sauce, and cornstarch mixture. Bring to a boil and cook until sauce thickens. Serve immediately.

Serves 4 to 6 with other dishes.

DRY-FRIED SHRIMP

"Dry-frying" is a particular form of stir-frying with a minimum of sauce. Use only enough liquid to gather the flavoring ingredients into a sauce, and then boil it away, leaving the seasonings clinging to the shrimp. With small shrimp (40 to 60 per pound or smaller), you can eat them shell and all; with larger ones, peel them after cooking.

- ½ pound small or medium shrimp in shell
- 1 tablespoon Shaoxing wine or dry sherry
- 1 teaspoon kosher salt
- 4 slices ginger
- 4 cloves garlic, peeled
  Oil, for stir-frying
- 1 tablespoon soy sauce

1. Run the tip of a small knife or a pair of kitchen scissors into each shrimp shell from head end, cutting outward through back side of shell almost to end of tail. Devein, if necessary, leaving shells attached. Rinse well and drain.

2. In a medium bowl, combine wine and ½ teaspoon salt. Smack ginger slices with side of knife blade to release the juices, and add to bowl. Toss shrimp in mixture, and marinate for 30 minutes to several hours.

3. Pound garlic and remaining salt to a paste in a mortar, or on a cutting board as follows: Smash cloves with side of knife blade. Sprinkle with salt, lay blade over garlic, and, leaning on blade with heel of one hand, rub with a circular motion until garlic is nearly liquefied. Keep cutting edge laid flat against board, and raise fingertips to avoid sharp edge. Scrape up garlic paste with knife and transfer to a small bowl.

4. Heat wok over medium-high heat, and add oil. Drain shrimp, reserving any marinade. Add shrimp and ginger slices to wok; stir-fry until shells begin to turn pink. Remove ginger; add garlic paste, reserved marinade, and soy sauce to wok. Continue cooking until shrimp meat is opaque and shells are coated with sauce. Transfer to serving platter.

Serves 4 to 6 with other dishes.

DRY-FRIED GREEN BEANS

This dish works best with slim, tender green beans. The Chinese "yard-long" beans are ideal, or use regular string beans of no more thickness than a pencil. You can also substitute asparagus, and omit the blanching.

- ½ teaspoon each *light soy sauce and black soy sauce*
- ½ teaspoon *black vinegar*
- 1 tablespoon *water*
- ⅛ teaspoon *sugar*
- 2 teaspoons *oil*
- 1½ teaspoons each *minced ginger and garlic*
- ¾ to 1 pound *green beans, trimmed, cut into 2-inch lengths, and blanched*
- 1 teaspoon *toasted sesame seed (optional)*

Combine soy sauces, vinegar, water, and sugar. Heat wok over medium-high heat, and add oil. Add ginger and garlic; stir-fry until fragrant. Add beans; stir-fry until just heated through. Add soy sauce mixture, increase heat to high, and cook until nearly all liquid is evaporated. Transfer to serving plate and garnish with sesame seed, if desired.

Serves 4 to 6 with other dishes.

BOK CHOY AND RED PEPPERS

The sweetness of red bell peppers is a perfect foil for the slight bitterness of bok choy. The vibrant red, white, and green colors make this a beautiful dish to look at, too.

- 2 tablespoons *oil*
- 1 teaspoon *minced ginger*
- 1 large or 2 small *red bell peppers, seeds and ribs removed, cut into 1-inch squares*
- ½ pound *bok choy, in 1-inch slices*
- ½ teaspoon *cornstarch dissolved in 2 tablespoons each soy sauce and water*

Heat wok over high heat, and add oil. Add ginger, and cook a few seconds until fragrant. Add peppers and bok choy; stir-fry until just heated through. Add cornstarch mixture to pan and cook 1 minute longer. Serve immediately.

Serves 4 to 6 with other dishes.

BROCCOLI AND MUSHROOMS WITH OYSTER SAUCE

Oyster sauce is frequently used in meat and vegetable dishes from southern and eastern China. It goes especially well with the flavor of black mushrooms.

- 8 dried *black mushrooms*
- 1 pound *broccoli or Chinese broccoli*
- 1 tablespoon *oyster sauce*
- 1 tablespoon *light soy sauce*
- 1 teaspoon *cornstarch*
  Oil, for stir-frying
- 1 teaspoon *minced ginger*

1. In a small bowl, cover mushrooms with lukewarm water and soak for 30 minutes or until tender.

2. Trim bases from broccoli. If using Western broccoli, cut off tops and separate into florets; slice stems across into ¼-inch pieces. If using the slender Chinese variety, simply cut the whole bunch into 1-inch lengths.

3. Drain mushrooms, reserving soaking liquid. Remove the mushroom stems, and slice each cap into ¼-inch-wide strips.

4. Combine oyster sauce, soy sauce, and 2 tablespoons of the reserved mushroom liquid in a small bowl. Add cornstarch, and stir to dissolve any lumps.

5. Heat wok, and add oil. Heat oil almost to the smoking point. Add ginger and cook until fragrant, 5 to 10 seconds. Add broccoli and mushrooms; stir-fry until broccoli is almost tender but still crunchy. Stir oyster sauce mixture and add it to the pan. Cook 2 minutes, stirring to coat vegetables evenly with sauce.

Serves 4 to 6 with other dishes.

SHREDDED EGGPLANT WITH MINCED PORK

To prevent eggplant from absorbing too much oil, Chinese cooks frequently steam it prior to stir-frying or braising. Barbara Tropp, chef, teacher, and author of the excellent *The Modern Art of Chinese Cooking*, suggests baking it instead, which gives excellent results. Whether steamed or baked, the eggplant can be cooked a day or two ahead of stir-frying, and refrigerated.

- 1 pound *eggplant (preferably the Chinese or Japanese variety)*
- 1 teaspoon *sugar*
- 2 tablespoons *regular or dark soy sauce*
- 1 tablespoon *black vinegar Oil, for stir-frying*
- 2 tablespoons each *minced garlic and ginger*
- 2 *green onions, minced*
- 1 teaspoon (scant) *red-pepper flakes*
- ¼ pound *minced pork*
- 1 teaspoon *sesame oil*

1. Steam or bake whole eggplant until soft. Peel large Western-style eggplant, but leave skin on smaller types. Allow to cool, then cut or tear by hand into shreds about 2 inches long. Dissolve sugar in soy sauce and vinegar and set aside.

2. Heat wok over medium-high heat, and add oil. Add garlic, ginger, and green onions, and cook until fragrant. Add pepper flakes, cook a few seconds, and add pork. Stir-fry just until pork loses its raw color, add eggplant, and continue cooking until pork is done and eggplant is heated through. Add soy sauce mixture, increase heat to high, and toss to coat evenly with sauce. Sprinkle with sesame oil, and transfer to serving platter.

Serves 4 to 6 with other dishes.

MIXED VEGETABLES WITH ALMONDS

This dish of assorted seasonal vegetables with crunchy almonds would fit equally well into a Chinese or Western menu. Use seasonal vegetables, with an eye to contrasting colors and textures. Firm vegetables should be blanched before stir-frying; quick-cooking vegetables need no preliminary cooking.

- 1 stalk broccoli
- 1 teaspoon cornstarch
- 2 tablespoons each soy sauce and Shaoxing wine or dry sherry
- 3 tablespoons oil
- ¼ cup whole blanched almonds
- 1 teaspoon minced ginger
- 3 or 4 green onions, trimmed and cut into 2-inch lengths
- 1 red or green bell pepper, seeded and cut into 1-inch squares
- 1 stalk celery, sliced diagonally
- 8 to 12 ears Chinese canned baby corn, drained (optional)
- ½ cup sliced fresh mushrooms or 2 or 3 dried black mushroom caps, soaked in water and sliced

1. Trim base of broccoli stem. Starting at base, cut across stem into ⅛-inch slices. Continue slicing until top comes apart into florets. Blanch in lightly salted boiling water for 30 seconds, and transfer to a bowl of ice water to keep cold.

2. Dissolve cornstarch in soy sauce and wine, and set aside.

3. Heat wok over medium heat, and add oil. Add almonds and cook, stirring constantly, until almonds begin to brown. Remove and drain on paper towels.

4. Remove all but 1 tablespoon oil from wok. Increase heat to medium-high. Add ginger, stir, and cook a few seconds until fragrant. Add green onions, bell pepper, celery, and baby corn (if used). Cook 1 minute, stirring constantly. Drain broccoli and add to wok along with mushrooms and almonds. Stir-fry just until mushrooms soften. Stir cornstarch mixture and add to wok. Stir and cook until sauce thickens and becomes glossy. Transfer to a warm serving platter.

Serves 4 to 6 with other dishes.

A colorful assortment of Mixed Vegetables With Almonds adds up to an easy and delicious stir-fry. The miniature ears of corn are available either canned or frozen.

BROCCOLI WITH BLACK BEAN SAUCE

Blanching firm vegetables like broccoli ahead of time makes stir-frying them a matter of seconds. This is a dish you could serve alongside another stir-fried dish—you can practically turn it out in the time it takes for someone to take the previous dish to the table.

- ¾ pound broccoli
- 1 tablespoon fermented black beans
- 2 tablespoons Shaoxing wine or dry sherry
- Oil, for stir-frying
- 1 teaspoon each minced ginger and garlic

1. Remove tough bottoms of broccoli stems. Cut middle section of stems crosswise into ¼-inch slices. Separate tops into florets. Blanch for 30 seconds in rapidly boiling salted water. Drain, and rinse with cold water to stop cooking. (This may be done several hours ahead.)

2. Roughly chop black beans, and soak in wine for 20 minutes or so.

3. Heat wok over high heat, and add oil. Add ginger and garlic; stir-fry until fragrant. Add broccoli and stir-fry until heated through. Add black bean mixture, stir to coat broccoli, and serve.

Serves 4 to 6 with other dishes.

DEEP-FRYING

Frying, also known as deep-frying, is an important technique in Chinese cooking. In a sense, "deep-frying" is redundant, because without any other qualifying label, "frying" means cooking foods immersed in hot oil. In true frying, the food is cooked only by the heat of the oil, not from any direct contact with the pan.

Fried foods have gotten a bad name, but it is not all deserved. Badly fried foods can absorb a lot of oil, making them both unappetizing and unhealthful; but with good technique, you can fry foods with a minimum of oil absorption.

There really is no secret to good frying in any cuisine, East or West. The critical factors are the quality of the oil, its temperature, and the coating on the foods to be fried.

The best oil for frying is a clear, relatively flavorless vegetable oil with a high smoking point (that is, an ability to withstand high temperatures without burning). Peanut oil is the choice of most Chinese chefs. It is relatively expensive, but it can be reused several times, unlike some other oils. Corn oil is a close second to peanut oil in performance, and it is quite a bit less expensive. Cottonseed oil is one of the least expensive oils, but it is less durable.

TEMPERATURE CONTROL

Oil temperature is critical. For best results, the oil should be between 360° and 390° F. At this temperature, the batter or other coating seals almost instantly, preventing any further absorption of oil. Oil that is too hot can burn the outside of the food before the inside is fully cooked. The oil itself will begin to burn at over 400° F, giving a burnt flavor to the food. Oil that is too cool is equally bad; below 350° F, the food will absorb a lot of oil before it is cooked.

To control oil temperature, either fry in a thermostatically controlled deep-fryer or use a thermometer specially made for deep-frying and candy making. Whether the thermometer is of the straight-line or dial type, it should be easy to read, have a range up to at least 400° F, and have a clip or other way to attach it to the pan. Look for a stem long enough to sink 2 inches or more into your oil. Accuracy is also important. To test a new thermometer, place it in a pot of boiling water. At sea level, it should read exactly 212° F (at higher altitudes it will be approximately 2° F less per 1,000 feet of elevation). If it is off by more than a few degrees, return it and look for another.

To keep the temperature up during frying, do not try to fry too many pieces of food at a time. Watch the temperature: If it drops below 350° F and does not recover quickly, you are frying too much food for the quantity of oil. One obvious solution is to use as much oil as you safely and conveniently can. Be careful, however, to leave enough room for the oil to bubble up during frying. As a general rule, the frying container should be no more than two-thirds full of oil.

FRYING PRECAUTIONS

Frying does present certain dangers, particularly burns and oil fires. To avoid being burned by splattering oil, have all the foods to be fried as dry as possible. Gently lower foods into hot oil rather than dropping them from a great height. Some splattering is inevitable, however, so wear an apron, long sleeves, and long oven mitts whenever possible. Shielding yourself with a wok cover when adding foods also helps. However, do not cover a wok while frying; the steam released by the frying foods can condense on the cover and drip back into the oil when you lift the cover, creating even more splattering.

Prevent oil fires by never filling the pan more than two thirds full and being sure it is stable. A round-bottomed wok should never be used for frying without its supporting ring, and the ring is recommended with a flat-bottomed wok as well. Do not leave a pan full of oil unattended over heat.

PREPARATION PLAN

The following are the basic steps for frying anything from a dozen wontons to a whole fish in a wok. See also Frying a Whole Fish or Duck, at right.

☐ *Organize.* Give yourself plenty of room to work and have ready all the hand tools you need—cooking chopsticks for dipping foods in batter, a wire skimmer for retrieving, paper towels for draining, serving dishes, and perhaps a wok cover to shield against splatters. Another useful tool is a fine-mesh wire skimmer for removing tiny bits of batter from the oil before they burn. If food to be fried needs to be marinated or a batter needs time to rest after mixing, this is the time to do it.

☐ *Heat oil.* Set up the wok or other frying pan. Be sure to use the wok ring for stability, even with a flat-bottomed wok, and position the handle where it will not be bumped accidentally. Clip the thermometer to the side of the pan in a position where you can read it easily. Add oil to no more than two thirds the capacity of the pan. Increase the heat to high, bring the oil to the desired temperature, and reduce the heat to low.

☐ *Batter.* To coat foods for frying, Chinese cooks use everything from a simple dusting of cornstarch or flour to an assortment of elaborate batters. The following recipes use an assortment of Chinese-style coatings. Most Chinese batters can be prepared quickly while the oil is heating. Unless a recipe specifies otherwise, don't batter the food until just before frying. If the last step is a dry coating, keep one hand dry to handle the pieces after dipping. Handle them gently to avoid knocking off the batter.

☐ *Fry.* Start with one or two pieces if you will be frying many small items. If using a wet batter, dip a piece into the batter with cooking chopsticks, drain off the excess, and transfer it to the oil. Watch the temperature; it will drop slightly, but should return to the desired temperature within 30 seconds. If it does not, turn the heat back to high, let it return to cooking temperature, and try again. Adjust the heat and the number of items fried at one time so that the oil never drops below 350° F for more than a few seconds.

☐ *Drain.* Retrieve cooked foods from the oil with the wire skimmer. Hold the skimmer over the oil for a few seconds to drain, and then transfer the food to a plate or tray lined with paper towels to drain further. If you will be frying many items, transfer the cooked pieces to a low-heated oven to keep warm. Some wok sets come with a curved wire draining rack that clips over the side of the wok, over the hot oil. These racks are handy, as long as they do not interfere with your ability to reach all the frying foods.

☐ *Clean up and save oil.* Wiping up the area around the wok right after frying is easier than cleaning up cold oil later. Most frying oils can be used at least two or three times, often more, if carefully strained and stored after each use. When the oil has cooled enough to be handled safely, ladle or pour it through a filter of several layers of cheese-cloth (coffee filters are more thorough, but very slow) into a clean storage container. Seal tightly, and store away from heat. Oil can be reused until it has become noticeably dark or has a strong cooked smell. Most cooks prefer to keep oil used for frying fish separate from other oils and reuse it only for fish.

Step-by-Step

FRYING A WHOLE FISH OR DUCK

Frying something large, like a whole fish or duck, is not as difficult a task as it may seem, but it can be a little intimidating. Here are a few tips to make it easier.

1. *Use the largest wok available, but don't give up if the fish is taller or wider than your wok can hold. Be sure there is room for the oil to rise when the fish is added. Start with the oil at nearly 400° F; the bulk of the meat will bring it down quickly to 375° F or less. If the temperature drops below 350° F, remove the meat until the temperature recovers.*

2. *Use a large (8 inches or more in diameter) Chinese wire skimmer. Dipping the skimmer in the oil first will help keep the meat from sticking to it. If the meat will not fit entirely in the oil, ladle hot oil over the exposed parts. When one side or end is nearly done, switch positions. Keep ladling oil over the exposed side.*

FILLET OF OCEAN DRAGON

To the Chinese, a fish dish looks incomplete without the head and tail. But it is not always convenient to cook a whole fish. This dish presents boneless pieces of fried flounder on a "platter" of the fried fish frame. The head and tail suggest a whole fish, but the fillets are easily served.

> 1 whole flounder, large sole, or other flatfish, 1½ to 2 pounds
> 1 teaspoon kosher salt
> 2 tablespoons Shaoxing wine or dry sherry
>   Oil, for deep-frying
>   Cornstarch for coating, or batter for Phoenix Tail Fried Shrimp (at right)
> 2 teaspoons Sichuan Pepper Salt (see page 34)
>   Fresh coriander leaves or watercress, for garnish

1. Have fish cleaned and scaled. Check cavity for any remaining bits of blood or organs, and rinse thoroughly. Divide top fillet in half by cutting down through skin to bone along lateral line. Lift inner edge of one half-fillet, and cut outward (toward fins) with long, gentle strokes, scraping knife against bones and peeling back fillet. Cut through skin at edge of fins to remove fillet. Repeat with other half and on other side of fish. Do not discard bones.

2. Cut fillets crosswise into 1-inch-wide strips with skin attached. Sprinkle with salt and wine; set aside.

3. If using batter, prepare it as directed in recipe. In a wok or other deep pan, heat oil to 375° F. Dust fish frame with cornstarch and shake off excess. Fry frame until crisp and brown, drain, and place on platter. Keep warm in a 200° F oven while frying fish.

4. Dip fish fillets in batter, or dust with cornstarch. Fry until golden brown, about 5 minutes. Drain and arrange on top of frame, overlapped toward tail like scales. Sprinkle with Sichuan Pepper Salt and garnish with coriander or watercress.

Serves 4 to 6 with other dishes.

Variation Serve with Sweet and Sour Dipping Sauce (see page 36) instead of Sichuan Pepper Salt.

SESAME FRIED FISH FILLETS

This Chinese version of the familiar three-step batter uses sesame seeds rather than bread crumbs. If black sesame seeds are available, mix them with the white variety for an attractive coating reminiscent of multicolored beach pebbles.

> 1 pound fillet of catfish or other lean white fish
> 2 teaspoons minced ginger
> 2 green onions, minced
> 2 tablespoons Shaoxing wine or dry sherry
>   Pinch of salt
>   Oil, for deep-frying
> ¼ cup cornstarch
> 1 egg, lightly beaten
> ¾ cup white sesame seed
> ¼ cup black sesame seed
>   Sichuan Pepper Salt (see page 34) or Soy and Mustard Dipping Sauce (see page 36), for dipping

1. Slice fish crosswise into two-bite-sized slices, about ¼ inch thick. Place in a shallow bowl, sprinkle with ginger, green onion, wine, and salt, and marinate in refrigerator for 30 minutes to several hours.

2. In a wok or other deep pan, preheat oil to 375° F. Drain fish and pat dry with paper towels. Have cornstarch in one shallow bowl, beaten egg in another, and mixed sesame seed in a third. Dip a piece of fish in cornstarch and shake off excess. Dip into egg, then roll in sesame seed until coated. Fry until sesame seeds are light tan, 3 to 4 minutes. Drain on paper towels and serve with Sichuan Pepper Salt or Soy and Mustard Dipping Sauce.

Serves 4 to 6 with other dishes.

PHOENIX TAIL FRIED SHRIMP

"Phoenix tails" are the poetic Chinese name for crisp fried shrimp, with their curling pink tails suggesting the tail of that legendary bird. A thin cornstarch batter gives an almost transparent coating of crispness while sealing in the goodness of the shrimp. Water-chestnut flour, available in well-stocked Chinese groceries, makes an even more delicate batter.

> ½ pound medium shrimp (about 15)
> 1 teaspoon kosher salt
> 2 cups ice water
> ¼ cup cornstarch or water chestnut flour
> ½ teaspoon baking powder
> 3 tablespoons water
>   Oil, for deep-frying
>   Hot Mustard Sauce (see page 36) and soy sauce, for dipping
>   Sweet and Sour Dipping Sauce (see page 36) or Sichuan Pepper Salt (see page 34), for dipping

1. Peel shrimp, leaving only small tail shells attached. Butterfly shrimp by cutting along back side almost through to underside and unfolding. Remove vein, if present. Flatten shrimp slightly with heel of hand or side of a Chinese knife.

2. Combine salt and the ice water in a shallow bowl. Add flattened shrimp; soak for 20 minutes. Meanwhile, combine cornstarch, baking powder, and the 3 tablespoons water; stir only until blended.

3. In a wok or other deep pan, heat oil to 375° F. Drain shrimp and pat dry. Holding a shrimp by the tail, dip into batter just up to tail shell. Allow excess batter to drain, then slide into oil near edge of pan. Fry until meat is set and batter begins to brown, about 1 minute. If batter does not brown, increase oil temperature to 400° F. Continue dipping shrimp one at a time into batter and adding around edge of pan. Retrieve shrimp as they are done, drain on paper towels, and transfer to serving plate. Serve with a choice of dipping sauces.

Serves 4 to 6 with other dishes.

*Fillet of Ocean Dragon is a
fanciful Chinese name for this
deep-fried creation in which
the fish bones provide a "platter"
for the boneless pieces.*

A whole fish, such as this sweet and sour version, is always an impressive finish to a Chinese meal. When setting a whole fish on the table, place the head nearest the guest of honor.

SWEET AND SOUR WHOLE FISH
Northern China

Although we generally associate sweet and sour dishes with Cantonese cooking, this dish is a specialty of the north-central Henan Province. Carp from the Yellow River is the traditional fish, but any lean, mild-flavored fish will do.

> 1 whole rockfish, black sea bass, or other lean white fish, 1½ to 3 pounds
> ¼ cup cornstarch
>   Oil, for deep-frying
> 1 tablespoon grated ginger, for garnish
> 1 green onion, shredded, for garnish

Sweet and Sour Sauce

> 1 teaspoon cornstarch
> ½ cup water
> ⅓ cup rice vinegar
> 2 tablespoons brown sugar
> 1 teaspoon tomato paste
> 1 tablespoon finely minced ginger
> 1 clove garlic, finely minced
> 1 teaspoon soy sauce

1. Prepare fish as described on page 20. Score sides with diagonal cuts almost to bone, 1 inch apart. Dust fish liberally inside and out with cornstarch, rubbing cornstarch into cuts in sides. Shake off excess cornstarch and set fish aside for 10 minutes. Repeat cornstarch coating, again shaking off excess.

2. See Frying a Whole Fish or Duck, page 51. In a large wok or deep skillet large enough to hold fish, heat oil to 390° to 400° F. While oil is heating, prepare Sweet and Sour Sauce, and keep warm.

3. Carefully lower fish into hot oil with a large Chinese wire skimmer. If fish is not covered with oil, ladle hot oil over exposed parts, and turn halfway through cooking. Fry until coating is golden brown and a chopstick or skewer easily penetrates thickest part, 8 to 10 minutes for a 2-pound rockfish.

4. Lift fish out of oil, holding it over pot for 15 seconds or so to drain. Transfer to a warm platter, pour sauce over fish, and garnish with ginger and green onions.

Serves 4 to 6 with other dishes.

Sweet and Sour Sauce Dissolve cornstarch in ¼ cup of the water; set aside. Combine remaining ingredients in a small saucepan and bring to a boil. Reduce heat, add cornstarch mixture, and simmer 5 minutes. Check seasonings and adjust to taste.

Makes ½ cup.

Variation For an entrée for two or when you don't want to deal with a whole fish, the above recipe will work with a large crosswise slice or steak of a similar fish (the cut known as "sliced fish" on many Chinese restaurant menus). Eliminate the scoring step, apply 2 coats of cornstarch, and fry at 375° F. Half a recipe of sauce should suffice for a 1-pound slice.

SWEET AND SOUR PINEAPPLE PORK
Southern China

Sticky-sweet versions of this dish, loaded with MSG and food coloring, have given sweet and sour dishes a bad name. But the original idea was and still is a good one: tender cubes of deep-fried pork with stir-fried vegetables and unsweetened pineapple in a sauce more sour than sweet. Make an extra effort to find red (ripe) bell peppers for this dish as they supply the color that gives the dish much of its appeal. Prepare the Beer Batter 3 to 24 hours ahead.

  ¾ pound boneless pork shoulder or loin (equivalent to 1½ pounds thick loin chops or country-style spareribs), cut into ½-inch cubes
  1 tablespoon light soy sauce
  ¼ cup Basic Chicken Stock (see page 64) or water
  ¼ cup plus 2 tablespoons rice vinegar
  2 tablespoons dark soy sauce
  1½ to 2 teaspoons brown sugar
  ½ teaspoon white pepper
  2 teaspoons cornstarch dissolved in ¼ cup water
  Oil, for deep-frying
  2 tablespoons grated ginger
  2 cloves garlic, minced
  3 thick green onions, white parts sliced, tops cut into 1-inch pieces
  1 large or 2 small red bell peppers, seeded and cut into 1-inch squares
  ½ cup pineapple wedges (fresh or canned in its own juice), drained

Beer Batter

  2 eggs
  1⅓ cups flour
  1 teaspoon kosher salt
  1 tablespoon oil
  ¾ cup beer

1. Prepare Beer Batter 3 to 24 hours ahead of use. Toss pork cubes with light soy sauce, and marinate for 30 minutes. Combine stock, vinegar, dark soy sauce, sugar, white pepper, and cornstarch mixture; set aside.

2. In a wok or other deep pan, heat oil to 350° F. Drain pork cubes thoroughly and dredge in Beer Batter. Deep-fry until crisp and golden brown, about 3 minutes. Drain on paper towels; transfer to warm serving platter.

3. Remove all but 2 tablespoons oil. Increase heat to medium-high. Add ginger, garlic, green-onion bottoms, and red pepper; stir-fry until fragrant. Add pineapple and stock mixture, bring to a boil, and cook until thickened. Pour sauce over pork; garnish with green-onion tops.

Serves 4 to 6 with other dishes.

Beer Batter Separate eggs. Combine flour, salt, egg yolks, and oil; blend thoroughly with a spoon. Stir in beer; beat to a smooth consistency. Cover and refrigerate for 3 to 24 hours. Just before frying, beat egg whites to soft peaks and fold into batter.

CHICKEN WINGS WITH ORANGE-GINGER SAUCE
Southern China

East or West, fried chicken is a favorite dish. This dish was inspired by a delicious Cantonese-style fried chicken breast with a lemon and pineapple sauce made by Martin Yan, star of the PBS television series "Yan Can Cook." As an appetizer, individual sections of chicken wings are prepared to look like tiny drumsticks, fried, and served with a tangy orange sauce. An entrée version follows.

  8 to 12 chicken wings
  1 tablespoon each soy sauce and Shaoxing wine or dry sherry
  ½ cup cornstarch or water chestnut flour
  1 teaspoon baking powder
  6 tablespoons water
  1 large orange or 2 tangerines (enough to yield ⅓ cup juice)
  Juice of half a lemon
  ½ cup Basic Chicken Stock (see page 64)
  2 teaspoons finely minced ginger
  1 tablespoon brown sugar
  1½ teaspoons cornstarch dissolved in a little water
  Oil, for deep-frying

1. Separate wings into joints. Discard tips or save for stock. With a small knife, cut through tendons connecting meat to elbow end of upper joint, then push and scrape meat and skin into a ball at upper end. Remove any bits of skin from exposed ends of bones. Prepare middle joints in the same way, but remove one of the two bones in each.

2. Toss wings in soy sauce and wine, and marinate for 30 minutes to several hours. Combine water chestnut flour, baking powder, and the water; stir to a smooth batter.

3. Remove half the colored outside of the orange peel with a citrus zester or vegetable peeler and cut into long, thin strips. Squeeze orange, and strain out any seeds. In a small saucepan, combine orange juice with lemon juice, stock, ginger, and sugar; bring to a boil. Reduce by one fourth, stir in orange peel and cornstarch mixture, and cook until slightly thickened. Transfer to a sauce dish and keep warm.

4. In a wok or other deep pan, heat oil to 375° F. Drain wings and dip into batter. Fry a few at a time until golden brown, about 6 minutes. Drain on paper towels and serve with orange sauce for dipping.

Serves 6 to 8 as an appetizer.

Variation For an entrée, make this dish with a whole chicken breast. Skin and bone 1 large chicken breast. Split into halves, and slice each half horizontally into 2 thin pieces. Continue with step 2 above. After frying, slice chicken crosswise into ½-inch strips, and serve with orange sauce.

Serves 2 to 4 with other dishes.

CARAMEL-THREAD FRIED APPLES

In this popular northern Chinese sweet, fried apples are coated with a caramelized syrup and then dipped in cold water just long enough to cool the caramel. The timing is a bit tricky, as you must simultaneously make caramel and fry the apples. It might be helpful to have two cooks, one to fry the apples and one to make the syrup. *Caution:* Caramelized sugar is extremely hot; to prevent burns, once the apples are coated with the syrup, handle them with chopsticks, not fingers.

> 1 egg, beaten
> 2 tablespoons water
> ⅓ cup cornstarch or water-chestnut flour
> 2 crisp, tart cooking apples, such as pippin or Granny Smith Oil, for deep-frying
> ½ cup sugar
> ¼ cup water

1. In a medium bowl, combine egg and water; add cornstarch and stir to a smooth consistency. Peel and core apples and cut each into 8 wedges. Add to batter and toss to coat evenly.

2. Have ready at the table a bowl of water with ice cubes. In a wok or deep skillet, bring oil to 375° F. In a heavy saucepan on an adjacent burner, combine sugar and water and bring to a boil. While syrup is boiling, fry apple pieces a few at a time in hot oil. Transfer to a lightly oiled plate when done. Turn off heat under frying pan.

3. When syrup begins to turn color, watch carefully. When it reaches a light brown shade, turn off heat. (Sugar may continue to darken from the heat of the pan.) With a long-handled ladle, transfer about 1 table-spoon of the hot oil from the frying pan to the syrup. Add apples, stir quickly with a wooden spoon to coat apples evenly with syrup, and transfer all back to the plate. Serve immediately. Each diner pulls off a piece of apple with chopsticks and then dips it into ice water to cool and harden the caramel.

Serves 4 to 6.

PAPER-WRAPPED CHICKEN

Bite-sized pieces of chicken fried inside a wrapper of paper or foil are a popular Chinese appetizer. Marinades for the chicken can be complicated mixtures of condiments, or a simple combination like the following.

> 1 chicken breast half, skinned, boned, and cut into ½-inch cubes
> 1 tablespoon each soy sauce and Shaoxing wine or dry sherry
> 1 tablespoon grated ginger
> 1 teaspoon sesame oil Oil, for deep-frying

1. Combine chicken, soy sauce, wine, ginger, and sesame oil; marinate for 30 minutes to several hours. Cut eighteen 4-inch squares of baking parchment or aluminum foil.

2. Place a square of paper on work surface, one corner facing you ("south"). Place 2 or 3 chicken cubes across center of square. Fold south corner over chicken to ½ inch from north corner. Crease fold. Fold in east and west corners so that they overlap each other, and crease edges. Fold whole package toward north, forming an envelope shape. Tuck north corner into envelope and crease to seal. Repeat with remaining packages.

3. In a wok or other deep pan, heat oil to 375° F. Fry chicken packages, a few at a time, for about 1 minute (paper will turn golden brown). To make unwrapping easier, slit open each package along folded edge before serving. To eat, undo package with fingers and chopsticks, and eat chicken with chopsticks.

Serves 4 to 8 as an appetizer (2 to 4 pieces per serving).

FRIED TOFU

Deep-fried tofu can be served as a hot appetizer with a dipping sauce (see page 36) or seasoned salt (see page 34). It can also be used as a meat substitute in such dishes as Mu Shu Pork (see page 45). The first step of pressing the tofu may not be necessary if your tofu is firm enough; just drain it thoroughly. Softer Japanese-style tofu will have to be pressed.

> 1 package (7 oz) firm Chinese-style tofu Oil, for deep-frying

1. Drain tofu well. Wrap in a clean kitchen towel or several thicknesses of paper towel, place on a plate set in a sheet pan, and invert another plate on top. Place a 1-pound weight on top plate. Let stand 30 minutes, unwrap, and drain. The tofu will exude a lot of liquid. (May be done ahead of time and refrigerated.)

2. Slice pressed tofu into squares, triangles, or other shapes about ⅜ inch thick. In a wok or other deep pan, heat oil to 350° F. Fry tofu pieces a few at a time until puffy and golden brown, 6 to 8 minutes.

Serves 4 to 6 as an appetizer.

EIGHT-TREASURE DUCK

This is a very impressive dish akin to a French *galantine*. A whole boned duck surrounds a glutinous rice stuffing studded with crunchy and savory ingredients (the "eight treasures"). The duck is first steamed to rid it of most of its fat, stuffed, and then deep-fried to crisp the skin.

> ¾ cup glutinous rice
> 1 duck, about 5 lbs
> 2 tablespoons each *dark soy sauce and Shaoxing wine or dry sherry*
> 1 tablespoon brown sugar
> 3 tablespoons shredded *Smithfield ham*
> ¼ cup diced bamboo shoots
> ¼ cup toasted slivered almonds
> 2 tablespoons minced ginger
> 2 green onions, cut into ¼-inch slices
> ¼ cup fresh or frozen peas or thinly sliced snow peas
> 4 black mushroom caps, soaked, drained, and diced
> Oil, for deep-frying

1. Cover rice with cold water and set aside to soak.

2. Wash duck thoroughly inside and out; pat dry with paper towels. Set it on a large cutting board. Remove feet and neck, if present. Cut off wings at elbow joint. Remove large pieces of fat from cavity and neck. Reserve giblets. Bone duck as directed on page 82. Rearrange duck, breast side up, on a deep steaming plate (see Steaming, page 78) and steam until juices run clear, about 1 hour. Meanwhile, combine soy sauce, wine, and sugar in a small saucepan. Cook over medium heat until sugar dissolves, then remove from heat.

3. Drain duck thoroughly (juices may be reserved for another use). Brush duck all over with soy sauce mixture. Place breast side up on a wire rack in a cool, airy place and allow to dry 1 to 4 hours. When first coat of soy mixture dries, apply another.

4. Drain rice and rinse several times until water runs clear. Line a bamboo steamer basket with damp cheesecloth and spread rice in an even layer. Dice duck gizzard and heart; scatter over rice. Steam 30 minutes; transfer to a bowl. Combine with treasures: ham, bamboo shoots, almonds, ginger, green onions, peas, and mushrooms, and stuff into duck. Sew up vent and neck openings tightly.

5. See Frying a Whole Fish or Duck, page 51. In a wok or other large, deep pot, heat oil to 400° F. Place duck in a large Chinese wire skimmer and carefully lower into oil. Have wok cover handy to shield you from splatters. Fry 5 to 7 minutes per side, ladling hot oil over exposed parts of duck. Drain well after frying and serve warm, either cutting duck into crosswise slices or tearing into skin with chopsticks.

Serves 4 to 6 with other dishes.

Deep-fried packets of Paper-Wrapped Chicken are easily unwrapped with the fingers, revealing the tender, ginger-flavored chicken breast inside. Unwrapping them with chopsticks takes a little more practice.

FRAGRANT CRUNCHY DUCK
Southwestern China

There are many steps in making this classic duck from Sichuan province—the duck is first dry-marinated in a mixture of salt and spices, then steamed until tender, allowed to dry, and finally deep-fried to give it a crisp texture. Fortunately, the work can be spread out over several days, and the result is so delicious that it is worth every step.

> 1 duck, about 5 lbs
> 2 tablespoons Sichuan peppercorns
> 2 tablespoons kosher salt (do not substitute table salt)
> Dried orange peel, 1 inch square, minced
> 1 green onion, cut into thirds
> 4 or 5 slices ginger
> Mandarin Pancakes (see page 114) or Flower Rolls (see page 113)
> Oil, for deep-frying
> Sichuan Pepper Salt (see page 34), for dipping (optional)

1. Wash duck thoroughly inside and out; pat dry with paper towels. Remove feet, and cut wings off at first joint; head and neck may be left on or removed as you like.

2. In a dry skillet over medium heat, toast Sichuan peppercorns until fragrant. Add salt and orange peel; cook until salt begins to color, about 2 minutes. Transfer to a spice grinder or mortar and grind to a medium-fine texture. Rub salt mixture all over duck inside and out. Place duck on a deep plate or heatproof pie pan, and marinate uncovered in refrigerator overnight or up to 3 days.

3. Remove duck from refrigerator 1 hour before steaming. Set up a wok for steaming on a plate (see Steaming, page 78). Place green onion and ginger inside cavity of duck. Set duck in a deep plate or heatproof pie pan. If part of duck hangs over edges of plate, arrange a piece of foil to

funnel drippings into plate. Steam 2 hours, removing accumulated juices every 30 minutes or so with a bulb baster. Save juices for another use.

4. Remove duck from steamer and drain thoroughly. If frying duck the same day, allow to dry at least 1 hour at room temperature, either on a rack or by hanging in a drafty place (see How to Air-Dry Poultry, page 88). Otherwise, refrigerate duck on a rack for up to 2 days. Remove from refrigerator, allow to come to room temperature, and air-dry for at least 1 hour before frying, preferably longer.

5. Prepare pancakes or flower rolls as directed up to stage of final steaming.

6. See How to Fry a Whole Fish or Duck, page 51. Fill wok with oil to two thirds of its depth. Heat oil to 375° F. Have ready a ladle and a large spoon or long cooking tongs. Holding duck with spoon or tongs inside cavity, carefully lower into oil, breast side up. Fry 3 minutes, ladling hot oil over exposed parts. Turn duck over carefully and fry 3 minutes longer. Remove duck, tilting neck end up to drain cavity thoroughly. Steam pancakes or flower rolls. Increase oil temperature to 400° F, return duck to oil, and fry 2 minutes per side. Drain thoroughly, and transfer to serving platter.

7. To serve this duck in the traditional way, set it out whole; diners help themselves with chopsticks, tearing off skin and meat and folding it into pancakes or flower rolls. If you prefer, after showing off the whole duck you can carve it Western style or hack it into bite-sized pieces Chinese style (see page 19). No sauce is required, but diners might wish to dip pieces of duck in small bowls filled with Sichuan Pepper Salt.

Serves 6 to 8 with other dishes.

Dry-marinating, steaming, air-drying, and a final dipping in hot oil to crisp the skin result in the incomparable Fragrant Crunchy Duck.

Celebrations call for Champagne and special dishes, such as this spectacular smoked duck, whole steamed fish, and spicy Kung Pao Shrimp.

CELEBRATION DINNER

*Tea-Smoked Duck
(see page 92)*

*Mandarin Pancakes
(see page 114)*

Kung Pao Shrimp

*Braised Tofu With Dried Fish
(see page 74)*

Steamed Chinese Broccoli

*Fish With Black Bean Sauce
(see page 79)*

Rice

Seasonal Fresh Fruit

*Beverage Suggestion:
Champagne*

A fragrant smoked duck with crisp skin, spicy stir-fried shrimp, and a whole steamed fish highlight this special-occasion meal. With a little advance planning and organization, it's easy to serve a multicourse dinner like this one and still have time to enjoy your guests' company. This menu serves 6 to 8 diners.

PREPARATION PLAN

Organizing a multicourse meal is a matter of preparing as much as possible ahead of time and using the same burners, woks, and steamers for a succession of dishes. In this menu, the duck can be marinated, steamed, and smoked at a leisurely pace over the preceding days. Only the final frying is done at the last minute. (Fragrant Crunchy Duck, page 58, would go equally well in this menu.)

All the ingredients for the shrimp, the fish, and the vegetable dishes are cut up, marinated, and otherwise assembled before the guests arrive. As you sit and enjoy the duck as a first course, the braised tofu is simmering gently in its casserole, the already-cooked rice is staying warm in its pot in a low oven, and the broccoli is steaming in a bowl inside the same steamer you used to heat the pancakes. After the duck, you excuse yourself from the table for a few minutes, transfer the excess oil from frying the duck to another pot to cool, and stir-fry the shrimp in the same wok. Use the method for steaming broccoli for any firm, crunchy vegetable, such as asparagus, bok choy, or choy sum. The reserved juices from steaming the smoked duck, diluted with water to taste, may be used in place of stock.

Just before sitting down to enjoy the second course of shrimp, broccoli, tofu, and rice, put the fish, already arranged on its steaming plate and covered with its black bean sauce, in the steamer. Twenty minutes later, slip back to the kitchen, and bring the whole fish to the table, placing it nearest the guest of honor.

KUNG PAO SHRIMP

See the introduction to Kung Pao Chicken, page 43, for a note of caution on cooking chiles in *kung pao* dishes.

> ½ *pound raw shrimp, peeled and split lengthwise*
> ½ *teaspoon kosher salt*
> 1 *teaspoon cornstarch*
> 2 *tablespoons soy sauce*
> 1 *tablespoon black vinegar*
> 2 *tablespoons water or Basic Chicken Stock (see page 64)*
> ½ *teaspoon sugar
> Oil, for stir-frying*
> 8 *to 12 small dried red chiles*
> 2 *tablespoons each minced ginger and garlic*
> ½ *cup diced red or green bell peppers*
> ¼ *cup sliced green onions*
> ¼ *cup diced or sliced bamboo shoots*

1. Toss shrimp with salt, then with cornstarch; set aside. Combine soy sauce, vinegar, water, and sugar; set aside.

2. Heat wok over medium-high heat, and add oil. Add chiles, and cook until nearly black. Add ginger and garlic, cook a few seconds, then add shrimp, peppers, green onions, and bamboo shoots; stir-fry until shrimp are opaque. Add soy-sauce mixture, increase heat to high, and cook until sauce is nearly all evaporated.

STEAMED CHINESE BROCCOLI

> 1 *pound Chinese broccoli*
> ¼ *cup Basic Chicken Stock (see page 64), salted to taste*

Cut broccoli into 2-inch pieces. Arrange in a shallow heatproof bowl that will fit in your steamer. Add stock. Steam until tender but still crunchy, 10 to 15 minutes.

The Mongolian firepot is a traditional cooking vessel that is now used all over China, not only for cooking but for keeping soups warm at the table.

Simmering, Braising & Steaming

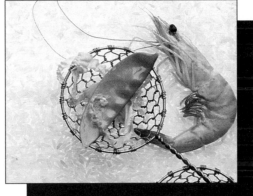

Meats and vegetables simmered in a rich broth, fish gently steamed over boiling water, clear soups full of finely cut ingredients—these are among the most satisfying of Chinese foods. Although we may think of stir-frying as *the* typical Chinese cooking technique, cooking with moist heat has a much longer history. Soups and stews were among the most important foods in China for centuries before cooking in oil became common. Steaming is an equally ancient technique, mentioned in texts that are over 2,000 years old. These techniques are just as important to today's cook in search of delicious, heart-warming food.

SIMMERING

Compared to cooking with oil and cooking with dry heat, moist-heat cooking is a slow and gentle process. Steaming, simmering, and braising work on the foods slowly, allowing an interchange of flavor between the ingredients and the sauce. This kind of slow cooking is especially good for tougher cuts of meat—shanks, necks, and other parts with more natural flavor than tenderness.

Slow cooking also gives the cook much more flexibility in menu planning. Unlike the neophyte who tries to fix two or three stir-fried dishes in a single meal, the experienced cook knows that a dish simmering or braising on the back burner will not compete for last-minute attention with a stir-fried or deep-fried dish.

Cooking directly in liquid is one of the most basic of cooking methods. In Chinese cooking (as in all good cooking) it is important to remember the difference between simmering and boiling. Actually, only a few foods, such as noodles, should be cooked at a full rolling boil. The rest—stocks, soups, and poached and braised dishes—are likely to be superior in flavor, texture, and nutritional value if cooked in liquid that is barely simmering.

STOCKS AND SOUPS

The foundation of most Chinese soups and many sauces is a good stock, preferably chicken stock. Unlike a Western-style stock, the typical Chinese chicken stock is made without a lot of carrots, celery, onions, or herbs. The result is a lighter, "cleaner"-tasting stock that is more versatile. By simply adding different ingredients, you can make anything from a delicate clear soup to a hearty one-pot meal of root vegetables and meat shreds.

Chinese-style stocks are either simmered directly over heat or steamed. Either way, the stock should never boil; boiling constantly agitates the stock, and the higher temperature causes some of the dissolved proteins in the stock to harden. Both conditions make for a cloudy stock. To get the clearest possible stock, some cooks prefer the more elaborate method of steaming. Both methods are described in the Basic Chicken Stock recipe (below).

Traditional stock recipes often call for a whole chicken, but if this seems extravagant, use an assortment of chicken parts. If you buy whole chickens and cut them up yourself, you should have a steady supply of backs, necks, feet, heads, wing tips, and giblets available for stock making. Freeze these "spare parts" until you have accumulated enough for a batch of stock. (Do not use livers for stock; other giblets are fine.) Also, do not use too many feet or the stock may be too gelatinous.

BASIC CHICKEN STOCK

> 2 pounds chicken parts, bones, or trimmings
>
> 2 green onions, roughly chopped
>
> 3 or 4 slices ginger

1. Wash chicken parts thoroughly. If using backs, remove kidneys (the two spongy pink masses alongside the backbone near the tail end) and any other bits of internal organs.

2. *Simmered method*: Place chicken parts in a stockpot and cover with water by 2 inches or so. Bring to a boil, then reduce to a simmer, and skim off any foam that comes to the surface. Add green onion and ginger slices; simmer 1 to 3 hours, skimming occasionally.

Steamed method: Place chicken parts, green onions, and ginger slices with water to cover in a deep bowl that will fit inside a large stockpot. Place bowl inside steaming pot, elevated on a rack. Add water to pot to a depth of at least 2 inches (bowl can be partly immersed). Bring to a boil, reduce heat so that liquid is at a simmer, and steam, covered, 1 to 3 hours.

3. Turn off heat and let stock settle a few minutes, then ladle or pour stock through a fine strainer. Leave behind the last ½ cup or so, which will be full of sediment. For a perfectly clear stock, strain through several thicknesses of moistened cheesecloth.

Makes about 1 quart.

RICH CHICKEN STOCK

Several soup recipes call for a richer stock, which can be made in one of two ways. The first is to add pork or veal bones and trimmings (beef makes too strong a stock for Chinese tastes) to the Basic Chicken Stock recipe. Increase the simmering time by an hour or more to extract additional flavor and body.

A second way to make a rich stock is to follow the basic recipe, but to begin with a previous batch of stock in place of water. The resulting "double stock" will make an excellent soup. If you cut up chickens regularly, this is a good way to keep a batch of stock fresh, and it gets richer with each extraction. Rich stock can always be diluted with water when a basic or thin stock is called for.

To Store Stock

Allow stock to cool, then refrigerate or freeze. Refrigerated stock may be kept two or three days, longer if brought to a boil for 10 minutes every other day. Frozen stock will keep for several months.

EGG-FLOWER SOUP

This is one of the simplest of soups, and one that can go with just about any menu. Keep the seasoned stock simmering on a back burner as you prepare the other dishes, then assem-·bling the soup is a 30-second process.

> 4 cups Basic Chicken Stock
>   (see page 64)
> 6 slices ginger
>   Salt and black pepper, to taste
> ¼ cup thinly sliced green onion
> ½ cup fresh or frozen peas
> 3 eggs, lightly beaten

Bring stock to a boil with ginger slices. Discard ginger, and season stock to taste with salt and pepper. Add green onions and peas. Pour eggs over surface of soup, allow to set for a few seconds, then stir to make "egg flowers." Serve immediately.

Serves 6 with other dishes.

CORN AND CRAB SOUP

Although corn is a relative newcomer among Chinese foods, rich, thick, chowderlike corn soups are now firmly established in the Chinese cook's repertoire. There are many possible additions to the soup, but crabmeat is the real favorite.

> 4 large ears fresh corn or
>   1 pound (4 c) frozen
>   corn kernels
> 1 tablespoon oil
> 1 teaspoon minced ginger
> 2 or 3 green onions, sliced
> ½ pound crabmeat, shredded
> 1 tablespoon Shaoxing wine
>   or dry sherry (optional)
> 4 cups Basic or Rich Chicken
>   Stock (see page 64)
>   Salt and white pepper, to taste
> 1 tablespoon cornstarch,
>   dissolved in a little water
>   or stock
> 2 egg whites

1. If using fresh corn, slice off tops of kernels with a small knife into a bowl. Scrape cut surface of cobs with back of knife blade to squeeze out milky hearts of the kernels. If using frozen corn, thaw and purée half in a food processor.

2. In a large saucepan heat oil over medium heat. Stir in ginger and green onion; cook until fragrant, about 30 seconds. Add crabmeat and wine (if used), stir and cook for a few seconds, then add stock and corn. Bring soup to a boil; season to taste with salt and pepper. Stir in cornstarch mixture, and simmer until raw, starchy flavor disappears, about 3 minutes.

3. Lightly beat egg whites until quite liquid but not foamy. With soup at a simmer, pour egg whites over top of soup in a large circle, allow to set for a few seconds, and stir to form threads. Serve immediately, or keep warm up to 15 minutes.

Serves 3 or 4 as a main dish, 6 with other dishes.

Variation Use 1 can (17 oz) creamed corn and omit the cornstarch in the recipe.

Variation Substitute shredded cooked chicken or pork, cooked and peeled shrimp, or imitation crabmeat *(surimi)* for the crab.

Egg-Flower Soup is one of the most popular of Chinese soups. Easy to prepare, with clear, simple flavors that fit into practically any menu, it is a universal favorite.

Hot and Sour Soup has its roots in Chinese herbal medicine, but you don't need to be ailing to enjoy its warming, satisfying flavors.

ABALONE AND WATERCRESS SOUP

This soup is simple but delicious. If fresh abalone is unavailable or prohibitively expensive, the canned variety or "abalone-type shellfish" (see page 33) make excellent alternatives. You can also use conch, whelk, or similar shellfish in place of abalone.

- 4 cups Rich Chicken Stock (see page 64)
- 2 green onions, sliced diagonally
- 1 tablespoon minced ginger Salt and black pepper, to taste
- 6 ounces fresh or frozen abalone, drained
- 1 bunch watercress, trimmed and cut into 2-inch lengths

Bring stock to a boil with green onion and ginger. Season to taste with salt and pepper. Slice abalone as thinly as possible into bite-sized pieces and add to soup. Add watercress and simmer until abalone is just heated through. Serve immediately.

Serves 4 to 6.

Variation Add half a chicken breast, prepared as in Sizzling Rice Soup, with abalone.

SIZZLING RICE SOUP

Any thin soup can be served with sizzling rice cakes. This recipe demonstrates the use of finely pounded and minced velvet chicken.

- 1 boneless chicken breast half
- 2 to 3 tablespoons cold water
- 1 quart Basic or Rich Chicken Stock (see page 64)
- 1 tablespoon minced or grated ginger
- ¼ cup sliced green onion
- ½ cups sliced water chestnuts or bamboo shoots
- ½ cup peas or sliced snow peas Salt and pepper to taste Sizzling Rice Cakes (see page 104), freshly cooked

1. Place chicken breast skin side down (the side with the smooth membranes) on cutting board. With the flat side of a Chinese knife, pound the breast lightly 3 or 4 times to flatten it slightly. Switching to the dull back edge of the blade, pound the chicken lightly and repeatedly until the meat begins to look minced. Turn over knife into normal cutting position. Holding one end of the membrane against board with your fingertip, scrape meat away from membrane. Discard membrane or save for stockpot.

2. Mince chicken as finely as possible, using either a rocking motion or a lifting and chopping method (see Chopping and Cleaver Chopping, page 18). Periodically add water, a teaspoonful at a time, and continue chopping until mixture is light in color and fluffy in texture. Chill until ready to add to soup. (May be prepared up to 2 hours ahead.)

3. Have Sizzling Rice Cakes ready for final frying. In a saucepan, bring stock to a boil with ginger and green onion. Add other vegetables, reduce to a simmer, and season to taste. Stir in chicken and cook until meat loses its raw color. Transfer soup to tureen and add hot rice cakes. Break up rice cakes with ladle when serving soup.

Serves 4 to 6 with other dishes.

HOT AND SOUR SOUP
Northern China

This soup, which started out as a medicinal preparation, is one of the most popular soups in northern-style Chinese restaurants. As usual, there are many versions—thicker or thinner, with or without meat, with other vegetables—but the basic flavoring should be peppery and slightly sour.

    4 cups Rich Chicken Stock
       (see page 64)
    6 slices ginger
    ¼ pound pork or chicken, in
       matchstick strips (optional)
    ¼ cup each shredded carrots
       and Chinese cabbage
    ¼ cup sliced green onion
    ¼ cup (½ small can) sliced
       bamboo shoots
    2 large black mushrooms,
       soaked, drained, stems
       removed, and sliced
    ¼ cup each cloud ears and lily
       buds, soaked and drained
    1 cake firm or regular tofu,
       diced
    2 tablespoons black vinegar,
       or to taste
    3 tablespoons soy sauce
    ¼ teaspoon black pepper
    1 tablespoon cornstarch
       Salt and pepper, to taste
    ½ cup peas
    2 eggs, lightly beaten

1. Bring stock to a boil with ginger slices. Discard ginger. Add meat strips (if used), carrots, cabbage, green onions, bamboo shoots, mushrooms, cloud ears, lily buds, and tofu; simmer until meat is done and vegetables are heated through, about 4 minutes.

2. In a small bowl combine vinegar, soy sauce, pepper, and cornstarch; stir to dissolve cornstarch. Add to soup and cook until raw starch flavor disappears, about 2 minutes. Adjust seasoning, if necessary, with salt, pepper, or additional black vinegar. Add peas. Pour eggs over surface of soup, allow to set for a few seconds. Stir to make "egg flowers." Serve immediately.

Serves 3 or 4 as a main dish, 6 with other dishes.

RED-COOKING AND WHITE-COOKING

Chinese simmered foods are classified as either "red-cooked" or "white-cooked," depending on whether or not soy sauce is used. But the distinction covers more than just differences in color. For example, in Red-Cooked Chicken (see page 77), a whole bird is simmered in a fragrant mixture of soy sauce, wine, fresh ginger, and spices, giving a distinctive aroma to the meat and a lovely red-brown color to the skin. White-Cooked Chicken is cooked in a more simply seasoned liquid, to preserve the natural color and flavor of the chicken. Each technique has its place in Chinese cooking.

The simmering mixture for a red-cooked dish is sometimes called a "master sauce." Master sauces can be used over and over, and get better each time. Not only are they good for repeating the original dish, but sometimes a tablespoonful or two provides just the flavor boost needed for a stir-fry or a dish of braised vegetables. If you "red-cook" different meats and poultry often, you might wish to keep separate master sauces for each on hand in the freezer.

To reuse a master sauce: Skim off and discard fat. Add half the amount of sugar and aromatics called for in the original recipe and one fourth of the amount of soy sauce to the leftover sauce each time you reuse it. This keeps the balance of flavors about the same, and the fresh soy sauce gives the right color to the meat or fowl.

A typical white-cooking mixture is less complicated than a master sauce: a simple stock, perhaps with a little wine, or just plain water plus a few green-onion and ginger slices. There is no need to save it for the same purpose; just use it for soup as is, or for making a stronger stock.

WHITE-COOKED CHICKEN

Sometimes the simplest cooking methods are best. A plump, tasty chicken, simply simmered with only a few seasonings, can be the centerpiece of a family supper or the starting point for a variety of hot and cold dishes.

    1 large chicken, 4 to 5 lbs
       Water or Basic Chicken Stock
       (see page 64), to cover
    2 green onions, cut into
       2-inch lengths
    3 slices ginger
   12 peppercorns
    1 tablespoon kosher salt (less
       if using salted stock)
    1 to 2 teaspoons sesame oil
       Coriander sprigs or green-
       onion flowers, for garnish
       (optional)
       Soy-Ginger Dipping Sauce or
       other soy-based dipping sauce
       (see page 36)

1. Clean chicken thoroughly inside and out, and place in a Chinese clay pot or heavy, covered saucepan. Add water to cover, green onion, ginger, peppercorns, and salt. Bring just to a boil, reduce heat, cover, and simmer until tender, about 1 hour for a large fryer, 1½ hours for a stewing hen.

2. Remove chicken from broth, and drain. Strain broth and reserve for another use. Rub skin with sesame oil and set aside until ready to serve.

3. Chop chicken into serving pieces (see Cutting for Braising, page 19) and arrange on a platter. Decorate with cilantro sprigs or green-onion flowers, if desired. Serve warm, at room temperature, or cold, with Soy-Ginger Dipping Sauce.

Serves 6 to 8 with other dishes.

"Drunken" is the Chinese term for dishes cooked with an ample amount of rice wine. Authentic Shaoxing wine gives the best flavor to Drunken Chicken.

CHICKEN SALAD

Although the Chinese do eat cold chicken dishes, "Chinese chicken salad" is strictly a Chinese-American invention. It is, however, very popular in restaurants here. The chicken can be steamed, "red-cooked," or "white-cooked." For a hotter version, use chile oil in place of all or part of the sesame oil.

- 1½ tablespoons *soy sauce*
- 1 tablespoon each *peanut and sesame oil*
- 2 teaspoons *black vinegar*
  Pinch of *sugar* (optional)
  Oil, for deep-frying
- 2 ounces *bean threads* (see page 107)
- 1 large *chicken breast* or *2 legs, poached or steamed*
- 2 *green onions, shredded*
- 1 tablespoon *shredded ginger*
- 3 stalks *celery, cut in thin diagonal slices*
  Large leaves of lettuce or Chinese cabbage
  Coriander sprigs, for garnish

1. In a medium bowl combine soy sauce, oils, vinegar, and sugar (if used); set aside for at least 15 minutes to allow flavors to develop.

2. In a wok or other deep pan, heat oil to 375° to 400° F; add bean threads. They will rise instantly and form a loose disk. Fry about 15 seconds per side; remove and drain on paper towels.

3. Remove chicken meat from bones and shred by hand or with a knife. Toss chicken, green onion, ginger, and celery in soy sauce mixture. Line plate with lettuce leaves, and top with fried bean threads. Arrange chicken mixture on top, and garnish with coriander.

Serves 4 to 6 with other dishes.

DRUNKEN CHICKEN

This dish of cold chicken marinated in rice wine will naturally taste most authentic with genuine Shaoxing wine, so make a special effort to find the real thing. The first step of this recipe is the same as that for White-Cooked Chicken (page 67), although this recipe works well with chicken pieces—legs, breasts, wings, backs—as well as with the whole bird.

- 1 large *chicken, 4 to 5 pounds*
  Water or Basic Chicken Stock (see page 64) to cover
- 2 *green onions, cut into 2-inch lengths*
- 3 slices *ginger*
- 12 *peppercorns*
- 1 tablespoon *kosher salt* (less if using salted stock)
- ½ cup *Shaoxing wine or dry sherry*

1. Clean chicken thoroughly inside and out, and place in a Chinese clay pot or heavy, covered saucepan. Add water to cover, green onion, ginger, peppercorns, and salt. Bring just to a boil, reduce heat, cover, and simmer until tender, about 1 hour for a large fryer, 1½ hours for a stewing hen.

2. Remove chicken from broth, and drain. Strain broth and reserve for another use. Disjoint chicken, place in a bowl, and sprinkle with wine. Marinate 30 minutes to several hours, turning occasionally. Chop chicken into smaller chopstick-size pieces, arrange on serving plate, and pour marinade over pieces. Serve cold or at room temperature.

Serves 6 to 8 with other dishes.

RED-COOKED PORK SHOULDER

This is a comforting, home-style dish full of simple goodness. In feeling, if not in flavor, it might be called the Chinese equivalent of our Sunday pot roast. Leftover red-cooked meat can be reheated or served cold, or used in stuffings for dumplings or steamed buns. Be sure to reserve the leftover simmering liquid, or "master sauce."

- 1 cup *water*
- ½ cup *soy sauce*
- ¼ cup *Shaoxing wine or dry sherry*
- 4 slices *ginger*
- 1 *green onion, sliced*
- 1 teaspoon *sugar*
- 1 piece of *pork shoulder, 1 to 2 pounds, with skin*

1. In a Chinese clay pot or other covered casserole, combine the water, soy sauce, wine, ginger, green onion, and sugar; bring to a boil.

2. Remove excess fat from pork shoulder, but leave skin attached. Add pork to pot and, as liquid returns to a boil, baste any exposed parts of meat with liquid. Reduce heat, cover, and simmer until meat is tender enough to pull apart with chopsticks, about 2 hours. Turn meat once or twice during cooking. Serve hot or warm.

Serves 6 to 8 with other dishes.

Variation Add bite-sized pieces of firm vegetables, such as carrots, turnips, or kohlrabi, to the liquid for the last 20 minutes of simmering.

Variation Add soaked and drained bean threads for the last 10 minutes of simmering. Serve in individual bowls topped with meat.

Red-Cooked Beef Follow the procedure for Red-Cooked Pork Shoulder, above, substituting 2-inch cubes of beef chuck or oxtails for the pork. Increase cooking time to 3 hours. Red-cooked beef is especially good served with fresh rice noodles (see page 106).

FIREPOT COOKING

The firepot or hot pot is China's equivalent of the fondue pot, a communal do-it-yourself cooking vessel. Of Mongolian origin, the firepot (see photo, opposite page) looks like a baker's tube pan with a chimney running up the middle. Meats or fish, noodles, and vegetables simmer in a hot broth, kept warm by a fire at the base of the chimney. Diners help themselves, transferring the ingredients a bite or two at a time to their soup bowls with chopsticks or special small skimmers. The noodles may be eaten along with the other foods or saved for the end. When all the ingredients are gone, the broth, reinforced by the food cooked in it, is ladled into soup bowls.

Firepots made of brass, copper, or stainless steel are sold in well-stocked Chinese stores. The traditional heat source is a lump of glowing charcoal, but for indoor cooking many Chinese use a portable bottled-gas burner.

Other tabletop cookers can be used in place of the traditional firepot. An electric skillet or electric wok is ideal, as the temperature can be easily controlled. Chafing dishes will also work, as long as they are deep enough. Fondue pots are not especially good for this use, as their typically narrow openings restrict the number of things that can be cooked at a time; however, you may be able to use the heating base of a fondue pot together with a shallower flame-proof casserole.

In one form of firepot cooking (see Banquet Firepot, at right), the uncooked ingredients are arranged on platters to be cooked at the table. Each diner picks up an ingredient with chopsticks and transfers it to firepot, retrieving it with the chopsticks or a small skimmer when done to taste. Each bite is then dipped in a sauce mixed to taste in one's soup bowl from a variety of condiments.

Another, simpler method is to assemble all the ingredients in the firepot first and cook them all at once, as in Lamb Firepot With Turnips at right.

All that is really needed in the way of a place setting is a pair of chopsticks and a bowl. For a more elaborate setting, you might include a plate, a separate small dish for the dipping sauce, and two sets of chopsticks, one for cooking and one for eating.

Just about any combination of meats and vegetables can be served this way; the following are a couple of possibilities.

LAMB FIREPOT WITH TURNIPS

In this version of firepot cooking, the whole dish is assembled in the kitchen, and then brought simmering to the table. Step 1 is optional, but gives a fuller-flavored stock.

> 3 to 4 cups Basic Chicken Stock (see page 64)
> Bones and trimmings from lamb (optional)
> Salt
> 1 bunch leeks, trimmed, washed, and sliced (save trimmings for stock, if desired)
> ½ pound bean threads, soaked until soft, and drained
> ½ pound small turnips, peeled and sliced
> ½ pound boneless lamb leg or shoulder, sliced across the grain into 1- by 2- by ⅛-inch pieces
> Soy sauce
> Hot Mustard Sauce (see page 36)

1. *If a more flavorful stock is desired:* In a saucepan combine stock, lamb bones, and leek trimmings. Bring to a boil, simmer 30 minutes to 2 hours, and strain. Discard bones and trimmings; skim fat from surface. (This may be done ahead of time and held for use.)

2. Bring stock to a boil in a saucepan and reduce heat so that liquid is at a simmer. Salt to taste.

3. Place bean threads in firepot. Scatter leeks, turnips, and lamb slices over bean threads. Pour in simmering stock. Transfer to table and begin eating as soon as lamb slices are done to taste. Combine soy sauce and Hot Mustard Sauce to taste for a dipping sauce.

Serves 4.

BANQUET FIREPOT

Firepot dishes can be as simple or as elaborate as you like. Ten or more ingredients is not unusual, and mixing fish, fowl, and meat is typical.

> ½ pound fillet of lean white fish (rockfish, snapper, flounder, halibut)
> ½ pound boneless tender beef or pork loin
> 1 whole chicken breast, boned and skinned
> 2 pork or lamb kidneys
> ½ pound small raw shrimp, peeled and deveined
> 1 package fried tofu or firm fresh tofu, well drained and cut into cubes
> ½ pound mushrooms, sliced if large, whole if small
> ½ pound snow peas
> 1 cup sliced bamboo shoots or water chestnuts
> 1 cup green onions, in 2-inch lengths
> ½ pound bean threads (see page 107), soaked until soft and cut into 6-inch lengths
> ½ pound Chinese cabbage, thinly sliced
> 8 cups Basic Chicken Stock (see page 64), salted to taste
> Dipping sauces: soy sauce, sesame oil, black vinegar, chile oil or Chinese chile sauce, minced or grated ginger, sugar

1. Slice fish, meats, and chicken breast as thinly as possible (partially freezing them first helps), then cut into 1- by 2-inch pieces. Split kidneys, remove tubes and veins, and slice thinly. Arrange slices along with shrimp, tofu and vegetables in an attractive pattern on platters (several platters may be needed for foods to be within reach of all diners).

2. Bring stock to a boil in firepot, or heat separately on stove and transfer to pot. Adjust heat so stock just simmers. Drain bean threads and place in firepot with cabbage.

3. Diners cook individual ingredients in simmering stock until done to taste, then season bites with a dipping sauce blended to taste. Ladle broth into bowls at end of meal.

Serves 8.

Variations In addition to or instead of the ingredients listed above, try any of the following.

Shellfish Scallops, sliced if large; squid, cleaned and cut up; shucked oysters or clams; lobster tail meat, sliced; crayfish tails; dried squid or scallops, soaked until soft and sliced.

Fish Fish balls (available in Chinese stores, or make your own from lean white fish ground to a paste and lightly seasoned; poach separately in advance to reduce cooking time).

Meats and Poultry Beef or veal liver; chicken or duck giblets; mild-flavored ham (but not Smithfield); meatballs of pork, beef, or veal, poached in advance; sliced duck breast; smoked chicken or turkey.

Vegetables Just about anything. Slice firmer vegetables thinly, tear leafy vegetables into larger pieces. Cylindrical vegetables such as carrots or daikon (a large, white radish) may be carved into decorative shapes before slicing.

Firepot dishes can be simple, with only a single meat or seafood plus a few vegetables, or fancy, as in this Banquet Firepot. Individual Chinese wire skimmers allow diners to retrieve their tidbits as soon as they are done. Enjoy the flavored broth as a soup at the end of the meal.

A Chinese clay pot is an ideal cooking vessel for Lions' Heads, large meat-balls with "manes" of cabbage leaves. However, any heavy flameproof, covered casserole of similar size will do.

BRAISING

Braising, or stewing, is a hybrid cooking technique combining elements of simmering and steaming; that is, foods are cooked in a covered pot, but not necessarily immersed in liquid. Often, the foods are lightly browned in oil before being cooked in liquid.

The ideal braising pot is heavy enough to hold heat and distribute it evenly, is able to withstand direct heat, and has a tight-fitting cover. The Chinese perfected just such a design a few thousand years ago, and the earthenware casserole known as a clay pot or sand pot is virtually unchanged today. With its sand-colored, unglazed exterior and dark brown interior glaze, this pot is ideal for slow cooking over very low heat. The most common design, available in various sizes, is about two thirds as tall as it is wide, with rounded or sloping sides. It may have one long handle or two short loop handles, and may or may not be reinforced with wire on the outside. A 3-quart pot, big enough to hold a whole chicken, is the most useful size.

Chinese clay pots are fragile, but they can safely be used if you follow a few basic rules. First, never heat the pot empty; it must be partially filled with liquid. Second, heat it gradually; start with low heat until the pot is warm, and then increase the heat to medium if needed. If cooking on an electric burner, use a heat diffuser to raise the pot up off the heating coils. Also, to avoid breakage, never put a hot clay pot on a wet or cold surface; allow it to cool first.

When a braising recipe calls for an initial stir-frying or browning, this is not done in the clay pot; the high heat could break the pot. Brown the food in a wok or skillet.

A clay pot is not necessary for Chinese-style braising. Any flame-proof casserole with a tight-fitting lid will work. Western-style cookware made of enameled cast iron, heat-proof glass, or similar materials will work fine. (Unglazed brick-colored "chicken bakers" are not a substitute, because they cannot stand direct heat.) You can also braise in a wok, but part of the appeal of braised food in a Chinese menu is that they free the wok for last-minute cooking of stir-fries and other dishes.

LIONS' HEADS
Eastern China

One of the most famous dishes of the lower Yangtze River region, this dish has a typically playful Chinese name—each large meatball is supposed to resemble a lion's head with a cabbage leaf mane. The meatballs are traditionally made with pork belly (fresh bacon); if that amount of fat seems frightening, try this adaptation made with somewhat leaner pork shoulder. Don't reduce the fat any further, however, or the meatballs will be dry.

> 1½ pounds boneless pork, about 20 percent fat
> 1 tablespoon finely minced ginger
> 1 egg
> 2 tablespoons soy sauce
> 2 tablespoons Shaoxing wine or dry sherry
> 4 teaspoons cornstarch
> 1 teaspoon salt
> 1 teaspoon sesame oil
> 1½ pounds Chinese cabbage
> 2 tablespoons oil
> 1 cup Basic or Rich Chicken Stock (see page 64)
> ½ teaspoon white pepper

1. Mince pork by hand, or grind on coarse setting of meat grinder. In a medium bowl combine pork with ginger, egg, 1 tablespoon each of the soy sauce and wine, cornstarch, salt, and sesame oil. Blend thoroughly. Roll mixture into 8 large meatballs.

2. Line bottom of a Chinese clay pot or other flameproof, covered casserole with several layers of cabbage leaves. Set aside 8 medium-sized whole leaves, and shred remainder.

3. In a skillet heat oil over medium heat. Brown meatballs lightly on all sides, and transfer to casserole. Scatter shredded cabbage over meatballs. Add stock, pepper, and remaining soy sauce and wine. Lay whole cabbage leaves over top and cover casserole.

4. Bring slowly to a boil, reduce heat, and simmer 1 hour. Serve in casserole, with a cabbage-leaf "mane" draped over each "lion head."

Serves 4 to 6 with other dishes.

BLACK BEAN SPARERIBS

Like many stews, these spareribs taste even better the second day. They can be reheated on top of the stove or in a bowl in a steamer. Serve with bowls of rice to absorb the delicious sauce.

> 1½ pounds thick and meaty pork spareribs
> Oil, for stir-frying
> 2 tablespoons each minced ginger and garlic
> 2 green onions, sliced
> 2 tablespoons fermented black beans soaked in 3 tablespoons Shaoxing wine or dry sherry
> 2 tablespoons dark soy sauce
> ½ cup Basic Chicken Stock (see page 64)

1. Have the butcher cut spareribs through the bones into 2-inch-wide strips. Cut between bones into individual pieces about 2 inches square.

2. Heat wok over medium heat, and add oil. Brown rib pieces, a few at a time, and transfer to 1-quart or larger Chinese clay pot or other flameproof, covered casserole. Add ginger, garlic, and green onion to wok, stir-fry briefly, and add to casserole. Add black beans with soaking liquid, soy sauce, and stock to casserole.

3. Bring contents of casserole slowly to a boil, cover, reduce heat, and simmer, covered, until meat is quite tender, about 1 hour. If serving the same day, skim off as much fat as possible from sauce before serving. Otherwise, refrigerate overnight and remove fat from surface before reheating. Serve in casserole.

Serves 4 to 6 with other dishes.

RED-COOKED SPARERIBS

Deep-frying ribs before cooking them in liquid produces marvelously tender and juicy meat with relatively little fat. This is one more example of the Chinese genius for combining several cooking techniques in one dish.

> 1½ to 2 pounds thick, meaty pork spareribs
> Oil, for deep-frying
> Master sauce from Red-Cooked Pork Shoulder (see page 69), or the following:
> 1 cup water
> ½ cup soy sauce
> ¼ cup Shaoxing wine or dry sherry
> 4 slices ginger
> 1 green onion, sliced
> 1 teaspoon sugar

1. Have the butcher cut spareribs through the bones into 2-inch-wide strips. Cut between bones into individual pieces about 2 inches square.

2. In a wok or other deep pan, heat oil to 350° F. Fry ribs, a few at a time, until lightly browned, about 2 minutes. Drain on paper towels.

3. In a saucepan or Chinese clay pot, combine master sauce (or water, soy sauce, and wine), ginger, green onion, and sugar. Bring to a boil, and reduce heat so that liquid is at a simmer. Add ribs; simmer until very tender, about 1 hour. Serve hot or lukewarm. Reserve any leftover sauce for use as a master sauce.

Serves 4 to 6 with other dishes.

EASTERN CHINA

The cuisine of the eastern coastal provinces and the lower Yangtze River valley reflects the rich food resources of the region. The river is the center of a vast network of lakes and canals in which fish, shellfish, and ducks are raised, and around which much of China's rice is grown. The seacoast provides abundant seafood. Tea is grown throughout the hilly parts of the region; Fujian province is especially famous for its tea. Zhejiang province is the home of the famous Shaoxing rice wine and of Zhejiang black vinegar, made from rice wine.

Eastern Chinese cooking relies heavily on simmering and braising. Dishes often include full-flavored liquid sauces based on long-cooked stocks. Red-cooking (simmering meats in a soy-based liquid) is a typically eastern technique. Wine is used more liberally in the east than in other regions. Rice wine is an essential part of red-cooking mixtures, and Drunken Chicken uses a generous amount of wine to marinate an already cooked chicken.

Eastern cooks are more likely to make complex sauces than are cooks in other regions. Steamed Fish With Black Mushrooms is a typical example, with its separately cooked sauce of mushrooms and minced pork poured over the fish after steaming. Even simple stir-fried dishes typically have extra liquid added and are cooked with a cover on the pan to promote an exchange of flavors.

In general, eastern Chinese cooking can be characterized as milder in flavor than that of other regions, and often sweeter. The complex but basically gentle flavors make it one of the easiest styles to match with Western wines. Red-cooked dishes go especially well with lighter, softer red wines such as Beaujolais or California Pinot Noir. A rich California Chardonnay is a good match for many of the region's seafood dishes.

BRAISED TOFU WITH DRIED FISH

The blandness of tofu makes this dish a useful balance to highly seasoned dishes. Depending on the rest of the menu, you can use more or less pepper or substitute red-pepper flakes. Serve over bowls of rice to capture the sauce.

> ½ ounce dried pollack, salt cod, or other dried fish
> 1 package (14 oz) firm tofu, drained and cut into ½-inch cubes
> 2 tablespoons oil
> 2 green onions, thinly sliced
> 2 ounces minced or ground pork
> 1½ cups Basic Chicken Stock (see page 64), seasoned with 1 teaspoon salt and ½ teaspoon white or black pepper
> 2 teaspoons soy sauce
> 1½ teaspoons cornstarch, dissolved in a little water

1. Soak dried fish in cold water until soft. If using salted fish, soak at least 24 hours in several changes of water to reduce saltiness. Drain and cut into ¼-inch pieces.

2. Place tofu cubes and fish pieces in a 1-quart or larger Chinese clay pot or other flameproof, covered casserole.

3. Heat wok or skillet over medium-high heat, and add oil. Add green onion and cook until fragrant. Add pork and stir-fry until it loses its raw color. Add mixture to casserole, along with seasoned stock and soy sauce. Bring gradually to a boil, reduce heat, and simmer 15 minutes. Taste for seasoning and adjust if necessary. Add cornstarch mixture; simmer 5 minutes more (can be held longer if necessary over very low heat). Serve in casserole.

Serves 4 to 6 with other dishes.

BRAISED ASSORTED VEGETABLES

This is another versatile side dish. Strictly speaking, only the carrots and broccoli stems are braised; the rest are simply simmered. Use whatever vegetables are in season, following the same procedure—firmer, denser vegetables (including most root vegetables) are cut fairly small and sautéed first; more tender and leafy vegetables are cut somewhat larger and need no preliminary cooking. Assemble this dish at your convenience and put it on the fire 15 minutes before serving.

> Oil, for stir-frying
> 3 or 4 slices ginger
> 1 cup carrots, slant-cut or roll-cut
> 1 large stalk broccoli, tops cut into florets, stems sliced crosswise
> ½ cup sliced bamboo shoots or water chestnuts
> 1 medium onion, sliced lengthwise
> 2 stalks celery, thickly sliced
> 1 cup Basic Chicken Stock (see page 64)
> 1 to 2 tablespoons soy sauce, or to taste
> ½ teaspoon cornstarch, dissolved in a little water

1. Heat wok over medium heat, and add oil and ginger slices. When ginger begins to sizzle, add carrots and broccoli stems; stir-fry until heated through. Transfer to 2-quart Chinese clay pot or other flameproof, covered casserole. Add broccoli florets, bamboo shoots, onion, celery, stock, and 1 tablespoon soy sauce. (Recipe may be prepared to this point ahead of time.)

2. Cover casserole and bring to a simmer over medium heat (low heat if using a Chinese clay pot). Simmer 10 minutes, taste for seasoning and correct if necessary, and stir in cornstarch mixture. Simmer 2 to 5 minutes longer; serve in casserole.

Serves 4 to 6 with other dishes.

RED-BRAISED DUCK

A little of this rich, satisfying stew goes a long way, especially when eaten home-style over a large bowl of rice. The duck may be braised a day or two ahead of time and refrigerated, but wait to add the noodles and cabbage until just before serving.

> 1 duck, 4 to 5 pounds
> 6 thin slices ginger
> 3 green onions, trimmed and cut into 2-inch lengths
> 1 medium carrot, sliced
> 4 dried black mushroom caps, soaked and drained (reserve liquid)
> 2 tablespoons kosher salt
> ¼ cup each soy sauce, water, and Shaoxing wine or dry sherry
> ½ teaspoon sugar
> ¼ teaspoon five-spice powder
> 2 cups shredded Chinese cabbage
> 2 ounces bean threads (see page 107), soaked in warm water until soft and drained

1. Wash duck thoroughly inside and out; pat dry with paper towels. Disjoint and chop into braising pieces (see page 19). Arrange ginger, green onion, carrot, and mushrooms on bottom of a 2-quart Chinese clay pot or other flameproof, covered casserole.

2. Heat a wok or large skillet over medium-high heat. Sprinkle with salt. Brown duck pieces, a few at a time, concentrating on browning the skin to render out as much fat as possible. Transfer browned pieces to braising pot. When all pieces are browned, duck will have rendered ½ cup or more of fat. Discard fat.

3. Combine soy sauce, water, wine, and sugar; add to braising pot. Sprinkle in five-spice powder. Bring to a boil, reduce heat, cover, and simmer until duck is very tender, about 1 hour. Remove duck pieces from sauce and set aside. Skim fat from surface (there may be ½ cup or more!), add cabbage and bean threads, and return duck to pot. Simmer 5 minutes longer, and serve in braising pot.

Serves 6 to 8 with other dishes.

SOY-BRAISED CHICKEN
Eastern China

This dish is a close relative of Red-Cooked Chicken (see page 77), but in this case the chicken is browned in oil before it simmers in liquid. The effect is quite different—less subtle but just as delicious. Serve over rice.

> 2 chicken legs
> 2 chicken wings
> ¼ cup dark soy sauce
> ¼ cup Shaoxing wine or dry sherry
> ½ teaspoon sugar
> 4 dried black mushrooms, soaked and drained (reserve liquid)
> 2 tablespoons oil
> 6 thin slices ginger
> 3 green onions, trimmed and cut into 2-inch lengths
> 1 medium carrot, sliced
> ¼ cup dried lily buds, soaked and drained
> 1 small piece (1 square inch) dried orange peel (optional)
> 4 points star anise
> Pinch of five-spice powder

1. Cut chicken legs and wings apart at joints, or chop into braising pieces (see page 19). In a small bowl combine soy sauce, wine, sugar, and ½ cup of reserved mushroom-soaking liquid; set aside.

2. Heat wok or skillet over medium heat, and add oil. Add ginger and green onion; stir-fry just until fragrant. Transfer to a 2-quart Chinese clay pot or other flameproof, covered casserole, covering bottom with an even layer. Stir-fry carrot slices until lightly browned, and transfer to casserole.

3. Increase heat under wok to medium-high. Brown chicken pieces, a few at a time, transferring them to casserole when lightly browned on all sides. When all chicken pieces are browned, discard oil and turn off heat. Let wok cool slightly, then add soy sauce mixture to deglaze pan. Pour deglazing liquid into casserole. Slice mushrooms and add with lily buds, orange peel (if used), star anise, and five-spice powder.

4. Cover casserole and cook over low heat until chicken is tender, about 30 minutes. Adjust heat to maintain a simmer, and turn ingredients a few times during cooking to coat evenly with liquid. Skim fat from surface before serving, if desired.

Serves 2 to 4 with other dishes.

BRAISED FISH WITH HOT BEAN SAUCE
Southwestern China

In this version of braising, slices of fish are browned and braised in the same pan, either a wok or a deep skillet. This dish is ideal for the thick, diagonal slices of rockfish or tilefish sold in Chinese markets. It can also be made with a small whole fish—as long as it will fit inside your wok.

> 1 large or 2 smaller fish steaks (about 1½ lb), 1 to 2 inches thick
> Cornstarch
> 2 tablespoons oil
> 3 slices ginger
> 2 unpeeled cloves garlic, lightly smashed
> 2 ounces minced pork (optional)
> 1 cup water, or ½ cup water and ½ cup Basic Chicken Stock (see page 64)
> 3 tablespoons Sichuan Hot Bean Sauce (see page 36)
> ¼ cup sliced green onions
> Shredded green onion tops, for garnish

1. Dust fish well with cornstarch and shake off excess. Put oil, ginger, and garlic in a cold wok or skillet, and heat over medium-high heat until quite fragrant. Discard ginger and garlic and add fish. Brown lightly on both sides and remove.

2. Add pork to hot oil and stir-fry until it begins to lose its raw color. Add water, Hot Bean Sauce, and sliced green onion; bring to a boil. Reduce to a lively simmer, return fish to pan, and cook, turning once, until easily pierced with a chopstick or skewer, about 5 minutes for 1-inch steaks. Serve garnished with shredded green onion tops.

Serves 4 with other dishes.

75

An assortment of warming, soothing dishes for a family dinner. A whole carved winter melon makes for an elegant, but definitely optional, presentation.

WINTER SUPPER

Red-Cooked Chicken

*Braised Chinese Cabbage
With Garlic*

Winter Melon Soup

*Green-Onion Cakes
(see page 114)*

*Beverage Suggestion:
Dark beer, ale, or stout*

*Here is a home-style meal
for a cold winter evening.
A whole chicken simmering
in a fragrant mixture of soy
sauce, wine, fresh ginger,
and spices gives its perfume
to the whole house. Warm
Green-Onion Cakes and a
garlicky cabbage stew also
help ward off the chill. In
true Chinese fashion, the
soup is not served as a
separate course, but is sipped
throughout the meal. This
menu serves 4 to 6 diners.*

PREPARATION PLAN

Not all Chinese meals consist of many dishes. A simple home-style meal such as this one may follow the pattern of a Western meal—main dish; side dish of vegetables; and rice, bread, or other starch. One-pot dishes combining braised meats and vegetables are also common; all that is needed to complete the meal is a starch and perhaps a soup.

Braised and simmered dishes allow you to put together a meal at a leisurely pace. In this case, the chicken simmers for a little over an hour, and can sit in its warm sauce for an hour or two longer. The cabbage also simmers unattended for the last 15 or 20 minutes, allowing plenty of time to roll out and fry the Green-Onion Cakes. With the broth preheated, the soup can be assembled five minutes before serving.

RED-COOKED CHICKEN
Eastern China

This succulent, aromatic chicken with its lovely red-brown skin is a classic northern and eastern Chinese dish. It can be served hot, warm, or cold. Chicken wings or other parts can be cooked in the same sauce and served as an appetizer or picnic dish.

> 1 whole chicken, about 4 pounds
> 2 cups each *water and soy sauce*
> ½ cup Shaoxing wine or dry sherry
> 2 tablespoons sugar (less if using a sweeter wine)
> 5 thin slices ginger
> 2 green onions, sliced
> 1½ whole pods star anise or 1 teaspoon five-spice powder
> ½ cinnamon stick, crumbled or ½ teaspoon powdered cinnamon
> 1 teaspoon sesame oil (optional)

1. Remove any excess fat from cavity and neck end of chicken, wash thoroughly inside and out, and pat dry with paper towels. Remove wing tips, if desired; otherwise, tuck them behind the back.

2. In a Chinese clay pot or other flameproof, covered casserole just large enough to hold chicken, combine the water, soy sauce, wine, sugar, ginger, green onion, star anise, and cinnamon. Bring to a boil, stirring to dissolve the sugar.

3. Slowly lower chicken into casserole, breast side down. As liquid returns to the boil, baste exposed part of chicken with liquid to start coloring the skin. Reduce heat, cover, and simmer 20 minutes, basting occasionally.

4. After 20 minutes, turn chicken over, being careful not to tear the breast skin. (The easiest way to turn the bird is with two wooden spoons, one inside the cavity and one outside.) Cook another 30 minutes, basting every few minutes.

5. Turn off heat and let chicken rest in sauce for at least 30 minutes or up to 2 hours. Baste frequently with sauce to ensure a deep, even color, and keep casserole covered to hold in heat.

6. Drain chicken thoroughly; serve hot, lukewarm, or cold. For an attractive shine, rub or brush skin with the optional sesame oil. Strain master sauce, and refrigerate or freeze for future use.

To Reuse Sauce Skim off and discard fat. Each time you use leftover sauce, add half the amount of sugar and aromatics called for in the original recipe, plus ½ cup soy sauce. This keeps the balance of flavors about the same, and the fresh soy sauce gives the right color to the skin.

BRAISED CHINESE CABBAGE AND GARLIC

½ cup lily buds
Oil, for stir-frying
1 large head garlic, separated into cloves and peeled
1 medium carrot, peeled and roll-cut (see page 16)
1 tablespoon minced ginger
1 pound bok choy or other large-ribbed Chinese cabbage, cut crosswise into 1½-inch slices
2 or 3 green onions, trimmed and cut into 2-inch lengths
2 ounces leftover Red-Cooked Pork Shoulder (see page 69) or Cantonese Roast Pork I (see page 87), thinly sliced into bite-sized pieces (optional)
1 cup Rich Chicken Stock (see page 64) or duck stock, salted to taste (see Note)
1 tablespoon black soy sauce

1. In a small bowl soak lily buds in lukewarm water until soft. Drain, squeezing out excess liquid. Cut or pinch off hard ends, and set lily buds aside.

2. Have ready a 1½-quart or larger Chinese clay pot or other flameproof, covered casserole. If using a clay pot, preheat it with hot water and dry it. Heat a wok or skillet over medium heat. Add a tablespoon or so of oil, and stir-fry garlic cloves and carrot until lightly browned. Add ginger and stir-fry until fragrant. Transfer contents of wok to pot. Add a little more oil, and stir-fry cabbage, green onion, and pork (if used) until just heated through. Transfer to pot. Add stock, soy sauce, and lily buds to wok and bring just to a boil. Pour over vegetables in pot.

3. Place pot over medium-low heat, bring to a simmer, and cover. Simmer 15 to 20 minutes, or until other dishes are ready. Serve directly from the pot.

Note Reserved juices from a steamed or smoked duck or chicken are ideal for this dish. Check for saltiness, and dilute as necessary with unsalted stock or water, bearing in mind that the soy sauce will add additional salt.

WINTER MELON SOUP

This is a soup of gentle flavors and textures. The mild, slightly crunchy chunks of winter melon flesh absorb the flavors of a rich chicken broth, and bits of ham, ginger, and green onion provide little nuggets of stronger flavor. This type of soup is a good choice to accompany highly seasoned dishes, or spectacular banquet dishes that should not have to compete for attention with a fancier soup. In a banquet, this soup is typically served inside a whole steamed winter melon, the rind of which has been decorated with carvings of dragons or other good-luck symbols.

4 cups Rich Chicken Stock (see page 64)
1 ounce Smithfield ham, cut in thin slivers
1 teaspoon grated ginger
Salt and pepper to taste
½ pound winter melon, seeded, green rind removed
2 green onions, sliced

Bring stock to a boil with ham and ginger. Season to taste with salt and pepper. Cut winter melon flesh into wedges, and slice each wedge ¼ inch thick. Add melon and green onion to soup; simmer until melon becomes slightly translucent, about 3 minutes. Serve from pot or transfer to tureen; in either case, ham will settle to bottom, so stir soup with ladle while serving.

STEAMING

Long before Western cooks discovered the benefits of cooking with steam, the Chinese were using this technique to produce delicately cooked foods. Steaming is an excellent method in terms of nutrition; whereas water-soluble vitamins might be washed away during boiling, steaming keeps vitamin loss to a minimum. Steamed vegetables also keep their color better than those that are boiled or cooked in oil. Steaming is also efficient; with Chinese-style stacking steamers, many different foods can be cooked at once over one heat source. But the greatest virtue of steaming is in the texture and flavor of the finished dish. There is no better way to preserve the delicate taste and texture of a perfectly fresh fish than to cook it gently with steam.

EQUIPMENT FOR STEAMING

Steaming apparatus comes in all sizes and shapes, but the idea is always the same: to support the food over a good quantity of boiling water, with room for the steam to circulate around the food. The size and configuration depends upon what is being steamed.

The first requirement of any steaming setup is a wide-mouthed pot that will hold a lot of boiling water. A wok will certainly work as a steaming base, but this is one place where the wok's round bottom is a disadvantage; it will not hold as much water as a straight-sided pot of the same diameter, and thus it may boil dry before the steaming job is complete. Specially designed steaming pots have vertical sides to maximize the water capacity.

The next requirement is a rack or other means of holding the food above the boiling water. Most wok sets include a steaming rack of some sort, either a cross-shaped wooden or metal rack or a circular, stainless steel ring that looks a little like a cake cooling rack. Another type of rack, sold as a separate accessory, is a perforated metal tray a couple of inches smaller than the diameter of the wok. Stacking steamer baskets of bamboo or metal are another option, with the advantage that you can steam several different items over one pot of water.

Fish, chicken, and other foods that give off liquids during cooking should be steamed on a plate or in a shallow bowl resting on the rack. The juices can either be used in the dish or reserved for another use. If possible, steam fish on the plate on which it will be served; this eliminates the danger of the cooked fish coming apart when it is transferred out of the steamer.

The last element of the steaming apparatus is a tight-fitting cover to keep in the steam pressure. Make sure that the cover will fit tightly over the food to be steamed before you bring the water to a boil.

All the steaming recipes in this chapter were designed for a standard 14-inch wok with a steaming rack and dome cover. This setup will easily accommodate a whole chicken or a fish up to about 2½ pounds; for a larger item you might need either a bigger wok or some other large pan such as a covered turkey roaster. Make sure that whatever pan you use can withstand direct heat without warping or damaging the finish.

For the steamed breads and dim sum beginning on page 111, you will need (in addition to the wok or other wide pan) one or more 12-inch bamboo steaming baskets with a cover, or their equivalent in metal. Most dim sum can be steamed directly on the steamer basket, without a plate. (Oil the basket lightly to prevent dumplings from sticking.) The lattice top of the bamboo steamer set, besides being decorative, allows some of the steam to escape, preventing water from condensing on the cover and dripping down onto the pastries.

Caution Steam can cause severe burns. When you lift the cover from a steaming pot, open it away from you and let the steam dissipate before reaching or looking inside. Long sleeves or long oven mitts can protect your wrists from steam burns.

STEAMING FISH

For the steamed-fish recipes that follow, use a lean, mild-flavored fish that will fit inside the steamer. The maximum size of fish is 2½ to 3 pounds for a 14-inch wok. (If you have a larger fish, try cutting off the head and steaming it first, then re-unite it with the body of the fish on the serving platter; remember that to the Chinese eye, a fish looks incomplete without its head and tail.)

Use whatever fish is fresh and locally available. Near the Atlantic, good choices for steaming whole include black sea bass and small striped bass; around the Gulf of Mexico, try red snapper or mullet; and on the Pacific coast, look for the smaller varieties of rockfish (locally called snapper or rock cod). Flounders and larger soles from all three coasts are also good choices. Among freshwater fish, try bass, perch, or catfish. Live farm-raised catfish and some other freshwater species are available in most Chinatowns.

The steamed-fish recipes can also be prepared with cut pieces of larger fish. Thick slices or steaks of halibut, tilefish, cod, or rockfish are just some of the possiblities. Fillets of any similar fish will work, too. But with these cuts reduce the cooking time to approximately 10 minutes per inch of thickness.

CLEAR-STEAMED FISH

This is the simplest form of Chinese steamed fish. The technique is called clear-steaming because it uses no black beans or other condiments, just the two essential fish seasonings: ginger and green onion.

> 1 *whole fish (about 2½ lb) or*
> *1½ pounds fish fillets, slices,*
> *or steaks*
> *Salt*
> 1 *tablespoon grated ginger*
> 2 *green onions, shredded*
> 1 *teaspoon sesame oil (optional)*

1. Prepare fish for steaming (see Steaming a Whole Fish, page 80). Sprinkle exposed flesh lightly with salt. Top fish with ginger and green onions, reserving some green tops for garnish. Steam until done by the skewer test.

2. Transfer fish to serving platter or serve from steaming plate. Spoon juices from plate over top of fish, sprinkle with sesame oil if desired, and garnish with green onion tops.

Serves 4 to 6 with other dishes.

FISH WITH BLACK BEAN SAUCE
Southern China

This is the classic Cantonese style of steaming fish. It works equally well with freshwater or saltwater fish and with whole fish, slices, or fillets.

> 2 *tablespoons fermented black*
> *beans, roughly chopped*
> 2 *tablespoons Shaoxing wine or*
> *dry sherry*
> 1 *whole fish (about 2½ lb) or*
> *1½ pounds fish fillets, slices,*
> *or steaks*
> 2 *tablespoons dark soy sauce*
> 1 *tablespoon each minced garlic*
> *and ginger*
> 1 *green onion, shredded*
> 1 *teaspoon sesame oil*

Combine black beans and wine, and soak 30 minutes. Prepare fish for steaming (see Steaming a Whole Fish, page 80). Combine beans and wine with soy sauce, garlic, and ginger, and pour mixture over fish. Scatter with white parts of green onion; reserve green tops for garnish. Steam fish until done by the skewer test, sprinkle with sesame oil, and garnish with green-onion tops.

Serves 4 to 6 with other dishes.

Variation Combining the Cantonese black bean sauce with the more typically northern brown bean sauce makes a less traditional, thicker sauce that clings better to the fish. Simply replace the soy sauce in the above recipe with canned brown bean sauce or, for a hotter sauce, a chile-flavored bean sauce.

Step-by-Step

STEAMING A WHOLE FISH

1. *Prepare fish for cooking as directed on page 20. Place fish on its side or upright on a heatproof plate that will fit inside your steamer (check to see that fish will fit inside steamer with cover on before heating water). If specified in recipe, scatter green onions, ginger, or other sauce ingredients over fish.*

3. *While fish is steaming, assemble remaining sauce ingredients. Some recipes call for a sauce to be separately cooked in a skillet or saucepan.*

2. *Bring water in steamer to a rolling boil. Uncover steamer, opening it away from you to prevent steam burns, and place fish plate on rack. Cover and steam until a skewer or chopstick easily penetrates thickest part of fish, 10 to 20 minutes depending on thickness.*

4. *When fish is done, accumulated liquids on steaming plate may be drained off or incorporated into sauce. Top fish with final sauce and garnish. Pull flesh away from bones with a spoon and fork and serve with sauce.*

HOT AND SOUR STEAMED FISH

Sauces for steamed fish can either be cooked along with the fish, as in Fish With Black Bean Sauce (see page 79), or prepared separately and poured over the fish as in the following two recipes.

> 1   whole fish (about 2½ lb) or 1½ pounds fish fillets, slices, or steaks
> 2   green onions, shredded
> 4   or 5 thin slices ginger
> 2   tablespoons soy sauce
> 2   teaspoons Chinese black vinegar or sherry vinegar
> 1   teaspoon sugar
> 3   tablespoons oil
> 1   tablespoon each *minced ginger and garlic*
> 6   small dried chiles
>   Fresh coriander leaves, for garnish (optional)

1. Prepare fish for steaming (see Steaming a Whole Fish, at left). Scatter green onions and ginger slices over fish. Steam until done by the skewer test.

2. While fish is steaming, combine soy sauce and vinegar in a small bowl and dissolve sugar in this mixture.

3. When fish is done, drain off accumulated liquid (if serving on steaming plate) or transfer fish to a warmed serving platter. Discard ginger slices. Drizzle fish with soy sauce mixture. In a wok or skillet, heat oil over high heat until a bit of ginger sizzles. Add minced ginger, garlic, and chiles, and cook until mixture is quite fragrant and garlic begins to brown. Immediately pour over fish. Garnish with coriander leaves and serve.

Serves 4 to 6 with other dishes.

STEAMED FISH WITH BLACK MUSHROOMS
Eastern China

In this dish the sauce will take nearly as long to cook as the fish will, so have everything ready before putting the fish into the steamer.

- 1 whole fish (about 2½ lb) or 1½ pounds fish fillets, slices, or steaks
- 3 or 4 ginger slices
- 2 green onions, shredded
- 1 tablespoon oil
- 1 tablespoon minced ginger
- 2 ounces minced pork
- 6 dried black mushroom caps, soaked in water until soft and sliced
- ½ cup seeded and sliced red bell pepper
- ½ cup Rich Chicken Stock (see page 64)
- 1 teaspoon dark soy sauce
- ½ teaspoon cornstarch
- ½ teaspoon sesame oil
  Fresh coriander leaves, for garnish (optional)

1. Prepare fish for steaming (see Steaming a Whole Fish, opposite page). Top fish with ginger slices and green onions, reserving some green tops for garnish. Steam until done by the skewer test.

2. While fish is steaming, heat oil in a skillet or wok over medium heat. Add minced ginger and pork; stir-fry until pork begins to lose its raw color. Add mushrooms (reserve soaking liquid) and pepper; stir-fry until pepper softens slightly.

3. Add stock, turn heat to high, and reduce slightly. Combine soy sauce and ¼ cup of mushroom liquid; dissolve cornstarch in mixture and add to sauce. Cook until slightly thickened.

4. When fish is done, drain off accumulated juices from plate and discard ginger slices. Pour sauce over fish and sprinkle with sesame oil. Garnish with green onion tops and, if desired, coriander.

Serves 4 to 6 with other dishes.

STEAMED CRAB

The only way to really enjoy crab is to eat it with your fingers, using slender chopsticks or the tips of the crab claws to dig out all the tasty meat. Provide plenty of napkins or damp towels at the end of a crab feast. See page 21 for more information on preparing a crab for cooking.

- 1 live Dungeness crab (1½ to 2 lb), or 2 pounds live blue crabs
- 1 tablespoon shredded ginger
- 2 tablespoons Shaoxing wine or dry sherry (optional)
- 1 tablespoon each soy sauce, minced ginger, and minced garlic (optional)
  Shellfish Dipping Sauce (see page 36)

1. Bring a large pot of water to a boil, and plunge the crab into it head first. Boil until crab stops moving, about 30 seconds. Remove crab from water and run under cold water to stop the cooking.

2. Hold crab by body and lift off top shell; set aside. Turn crab over and remove triangular breastplate on underside, together with soft spines hidden underneath. Turn top side up again and remove gray, feathery gills. Remove jaws and intestine, a crooked white tube running from front to back. Remaining spongy mass of tissue (olive green in uncooked crab, pale yellow when fully cooked) is mostly fat; reserve for step 5, if desired. Rinse body of crab until only meat and shell remain. Remove and reserve fat from corners of shell, and rinse shell thoroughly.

3. Split body down the middle, then cut each half between legs into 5 pieces, each attached to a leg or claw. Crack each section of leg and claw with one sharp blow of a mallet.

4. Place crab pieces and top shell on steaming plate. Sprinkle with ginger and wine (if used). Steam until shells turn red and meat is an opaque white, about 10 minutes for blue crabs, 15 to 20 minutes for Dungeness crab.

5. If you want to make a second, optional sauce, when crab is nearly done, combine reserved fat, soy sauce, ginger, and garlic in a small saucepan. Simmer until fat turns solid yellow and begins to separate. Transfer to individual bowls.

6. Transfer crab pieces to serving platter and arrange in a lifelike pattern, with shell over meat in center. Serve with individual bowls of Shellfish Dipping Sauce.

Serves 2 to 4 with other dishes.

FUZZY MELON WITH HAM

With its mild flavor and soft texture when cooked, fuzzy melon should be paired with foods stronger in flavor and of a contrasting texture, such as slivers of salty ham. Winter melon, cucumbers, and summer squashes can also be prepared this way.

- 1 pound fuzzy melon, cut into ½-inch slices
- 1 ounce Smithfield ham, shredded
- ¼ cup chicken stock

Place fuzzy melon slices in a bowl that will fit inside your steamer. Top with ham shreds and moisten with stock. Steam until tender, about 8 minutes.

Serves 4 to 6 with other dishes.

STUFFED BITTER MELON

Bitter melon, which looks like a bumpy, pale green cucumber, is aptly named. Its strong quinine-bitter flavor is an acquired taste. If you prefer milder flavors, this dish can be made with cucumbers or fuzzy melon, but skip the blanching step with these vegetables.

    1   bitter melon
    ½   pound boneless pork, finely
        ground or minced
    2   teaspoons minced ginger
    1   tablespoon minced green
        onion
    ¼   teaspoon kosher salt
        Pinch white pepper
    1   teaspoon cornstarch, plus
        cornstarch for dusting
        Soy sauce
        Sesame oil

1. Slice bitter melon crosswise into ⅜-inch slices. Remove seeds with a small knife or melon baller. Blanch slices in rapidly boiling salted water 1 minute, rinse with cold water to stop cooking, and drain thoroughly on a clean towel.

2. In a medium bowl combine pork, ginger, green onion, salt, pepper, and 1 teaspoon cornstarch; beat to a smooth consistency. Dust inside of melon slices with cornstarch, and stuff with a spoonful of pork mixture, heaping stuffing slightly above top of slice and spreading it out toward edges. (This may be prepared up to 4 hours ahead and refrigerated.)

3. Steam stuffed slices directly on a bamboo or metal steamer tray until stuffing is thoroughly cooked, 12 to 15 minutes. Serve with soy sauce and sesame oil for dipping.

Serves 4 to 6 with other dishes.

EIGHT-TREASURE CHICKEN

Like Eight-Treasure Duck (see page 57), this dish is a show-stopper. You can bone the chicken with the skin intact, as directed on page 19. Boning the chicken is not difficult, but it takes time, especially the first time. Don't worry if you cut or tear the skin in a few places; the leaf wrapping will hold it together. The other tricky step is tying up the bundle of chicken, stuffing, and leaves; another pair of hands is helpful. Use a plate to turn the package while tying the strings. Bamboo leaves are available in Asian groceries.

    1   large frying chicken, 3½
        to 4 pounds, with giblets
    8   large dried bamboo leaves,
        soaked in warm water
        until soft
    1   tablespoon each soy sauce and
        Shaoxing wine or dry sherry
    ¾   cup glutinous rice, soaked in
        cold water 1 hour
    1   Chinese sausage, cut in ¼-inch
        diagonal slices, or 2 ounces
        Cantonese Roast Pork I or II
        (see page 87), diced
    ¼   cup dried lotus seed,
        blanched, or whole blanched
        almonds
    2   tablespoons dried shrimp,
        soaked and drained
    4   dried black mushroom caps,
        soaked, drained, and diced
    2   tablespoons cloud ears,
        soaked and drained
        (optional)
    ¼   cup water chestnuts
        (preferably fresh), diced
    ½   cup sliced green onions
    1   teaspoon kosher salt

1. Rinse and dry chicken and set it on a large cutting board. With a cleaver, cut off wings at elbow joint. Cut through drumstick just above lower joint. Cut off neck, if present. Remove fat from cavity and neck.

2. Place chicken breast side down on board. With a sharp boning or paring knife, cut through skin along backbone. Peel skin back a little on one side, cutting away meat from bones. When hip and shoulder joints are exposed, twist or cut them away from carcass, being careful not to tear

skin. Leave leg and wing alone for now and concentrate on cutting the breast free from breastbone. Be especially careful not to puncture skin lying across breastbone. Repeat on other side, then lift carcass away from skin, carefully cutting skin free from ridge of breastbone.

3. Remove wing bones by first cutting tendons connecting meat to shoulder joint, then cutting and scraping meat away from bones. When most of bone is free, push wing inside out and pull bone free. Remove leg bones by a similar process, first cutting free thigh bone, then drumstick. You should now have left a whole skin and most of the meat. Trim any large pieces of meat remaining on carcass and add to skin.

4. Drain bamboo leaves and cut off thick stems. Cut two 4-foot lengths of kitchen twine, and lay them crosswise across bottom of a shallow steaming bowl. Lay two leaves crosswise over string in bowl. Arrange remaining leaves at intermediate angles to cover bottom of bowl completely. Combine soy sauce and wine; rub mixture over chicken skin. Place chicken skin side down in bowl on top of leaves. Rearrange any loose pieces of meat on skin to form a roughly equal layer. Drain rice and combine with sausage, lotus seed, shrimp, mushroom, cloud ears, water chestnuts, green onions, and salt (include diced gizzard and heart, if desired, but not liver). Spread mixture over middle of chicken, then wrap skin around stuffing, overlapping slightly. Fold leaves tightly around chicken and secure with strings. Tie bundle in several directions to maintain shape.

5. Steam in bowl, skin side up (the side with wider parts of leaves showing) for 2 hours. To serve: Remove strings and set package in serving dish, skin side up. Cut skin open with 4 crossing cuts, cutting down through skin into stuffing, and fold back leaves like an 8-petaled flower. Discard loose pieces of leaves. Spoon a little of stock from steaming bowl onto stuffing before serving.

Serves 6 to 8 with other dishes.

82

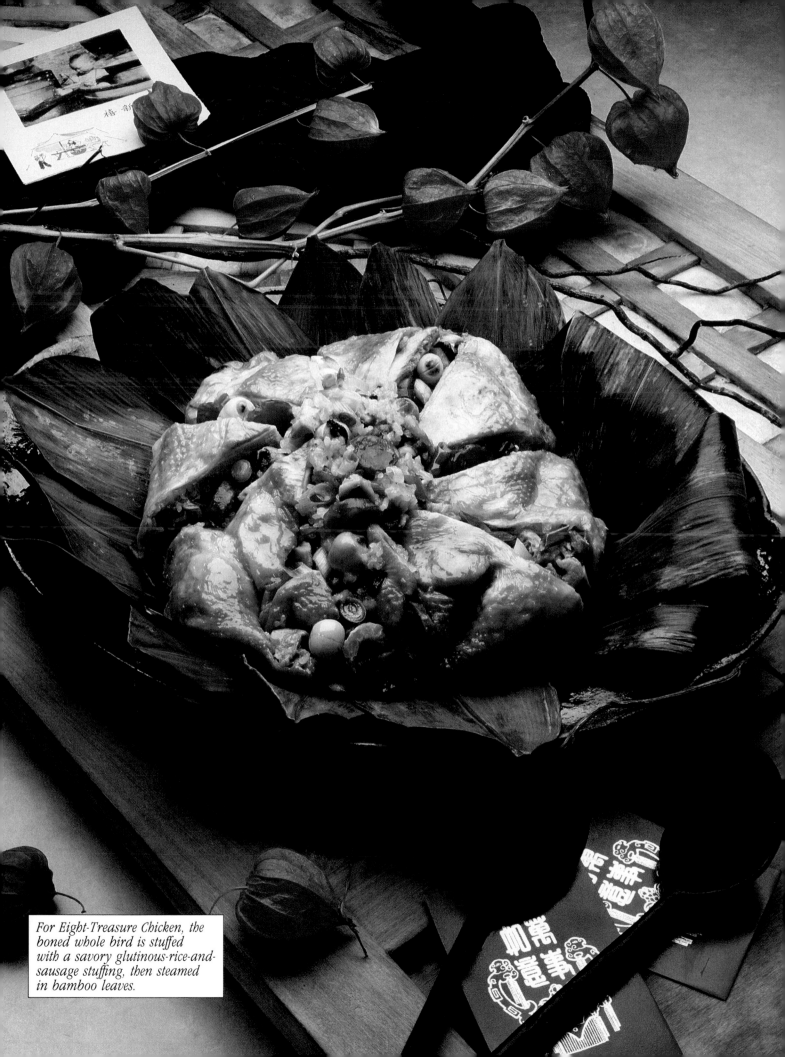

For Eight-Treasure Chicken, the boned whole bird is stuffed with a savory glutinous-rice-and-sausage stuffing, then steamed in bamboo leaves.

Tools and ingredients for dry-heat cooking, Chinese style: At top is a Mongolian barbecue grill; at bottom are ingredients for smoking poultry or fish in a wok.

Roasting, Grilling & Smoking

Dry-heat cooking dates back to prehistory, when food was cooked directly over a fire. As with every other cooking method, the Chinese have adapted it to various forms, each designed to cook particular foods with a minimum of fuel. Roasting is a large-scale operation that is for the most part left to restaurants, but the home cook has many ways of cooking with dry heat, including grilling, ''buried'' cooking, and an ingenious method of stove-top smoking.

Sweet, mahogany-colored Cantonese Roast Pork is used in a wide range of Chinese dishes, from stir-fries to fried rice and Cold Noodles With Assorted Toppings, above (see page 109).

ROASTING

The various methods of cooking with dry heat—roasting, buried cooking, smoking, and grilling—are used in Chinese cuisine primarily for pork and poultry. The amount of meat in the Chinese diet is relatively small, and it would be extravagant to use great amounts of fuel to roast large cuts of meat for hours. The dry-heat methods used in the home are generally done fairly quickly on top of the stove or on a charcoal brazier.

The traditional Chinese kitchen does not have an oven, so roasting as we know it in the West is not a common home technique. But roasted dishes do have an important role in Chinese cuisine. The difference is that most roasted meats are purchased cooked rather than being prepared

at home (just as the French buy their bread from a baker rather than bake it themselves). Restaurants and carry-out shops make more efficient use of fuel by roasting many chickens, ducks, and pigs at one time. Even in this country, many Chinese prefer to buy their roasted meats from a Chinese "deli" rather than going to the trouble of preparing them at home.

With a modern home oven, however, it's easy to roast meats Chinese style, as the following recipes demonstrate. Many of the dishes known as "barbecued" in Chinese are actually roasted in gas-fired ovens rather than in the traditional wood-fired ovens. Note that several of the recipes that follow combine roasting with another cooking method such as a preliminary simmering.

CANTONESE ROAST PORK I
Southern China

This is a home version of *char siu*, the reddish roast pork that is a standard item in Cantonese delis in every Chinatown. The marinade in this recipe gives the outside of the pork a beautiful mahogany glaze that is much more attractive than the commercial versions, which are typically tinted bright red from ketchup or even red food coloring. The meat is traditionally hung from S-shaped hooks for roasting, but unless your oven is unusually tall, this horizontal roasting method is more practical. Roasting over water keeps the drippings from burning and produces an especially juicy meat.

- 2 tablespoons oil
- 1 tablespoon each *minced garlic and ginger*
- 2 tablespoons *minced shallot or green onion*
- 1 tablespoon *Shaoxing wine or dry sherry*
- ½ teaspoon *five-spice powder*
- 1 tablespoon *red bean curd, with liquid (optional; see Note)*
- 2 tablespoons each *hoisin sauce and honey*
- 1 tablespoon plus 1 teaspoon *dark soy sauce*
- 2 pounds *boneless pork (shoulder, butt, or leg), in one piece*

1. In a small skillet or saucepan, heat oil over low heat. Add garlic, ginger, and shallot; cook 5 minutes, adjusting heat so that the mixture barely sizzles.

2. Turn off heat and stir in wine, five-spice powder, red bean curd (if used), and 1 tablespoon each of the hoisin sauce, honey, and soy sauce.

3. Separate pork along the natural seams, removing any large pieces of fat and gristle. Cut the meat along the grain into 1-inch by 2-inch strips up to 8 inches long. Toss meat strips in marinade to coat them evenly. Transfer to a bowl and scrape any remaining marinade from pan into bowl. Cover and refrigerate 6 to 24 hours in refrigerator. Remove from refrigerator 1 hour before roasting.

4. Preheat oven to 350° F. Place one or two cooling racks over the top of a roasting pan. Fill pan with water to a depth of 1 inch. Wipe excess marinade off pork strips and place strips across rack so that they do not touch one another and do not hang over sides of pan. Reserve marinade.

5. Roast 45 minutes. Meanwhile, strain marinade and combine with remaining hoisin sauce, honey, and soy sauce. Occasionally brush meat with this mixture as it cooks. Increase heat to 450° F and roast 10 minutes more. Brush meat with marinade after roasting to glaze surface. Serve hot or allow to cool on rack. To serve, slice thinly across the grain.

Serves 8 to 10 as an appetizer.

<u>Note</u> Red bean curd is a fragrant, salty, fermented form of tofu sold in cans and jars in Chinese groceries. It gets its bright red color from red rice, a natural coloring ingredient. If unavailable, add ½ teaspoon kosher salt to the marinade to compensate.

CANTONESE ROAST PORK II
Southern China

When you don't have several hours to marinate the meat, here is a shortcut method of making *char siu*. The meat is first simmered, then steeped in a thin marinade, and finally broiled to produce the characteristic roasted flavor. This also works well on an outdoor charcoal grill.

- 2 pounds *boneless pork (shoulder, butt, or leg)*
- 1 cup water
- ¼ cup *dark soy sauce*
- 2 tablespoons *Shaoxing wine or dry sherry*
- 1 heaping tablespoon *brown sugar*
- 2 green onions, *chopped*
- 3 or 4 slices *ginger*
- ½ teaspoon *five-spice powder*
- 1 tablespoon *hoisin sauce*

1. Separate and slice pork as described in step 3 of Cantonese Roast Pork I.

2. In a wok or large saucepan, combine water, soy sauce, wine, sugar, green onion, ginger, and five-spice powder; bring to a boil. Add meat strips and simmer 15 minutes. Turn off heat and let steep 30 minutes to 1 hour.

3. Preheat broiler. Remove meat from marinade. Combine hoisin sauce with 2 tablespoons marinade and rub mixture over meat.

4. Broil meat, turning as necessary, until outside is nicely browned, 5 to 8 minutes per side. Serve hot, warm, or cold.

Serves 8 to 10 as an appetizer.

BARBECUED SPARERIBS
Southern China

Prepared in the same way as the boneless Cantonese Roast Pork I, these ribs make delicious nibbling as an appetizer or as a side dish with other foods. Even if you are particularly adept with chopsticks, you will probably want to eat these spareribs with your fingers.

- 2 pounds *pork spareribs*
- 2 tablespoons oil
- 1 tablespoon each *minced garlic and ginger*
- 2 tablespoons *minced shallot or green onion*
- 1 tablespoon *Shaoxing wine or dry sherry*
- ½ teaspoon *five-spice powder*
- 1 tablespoon *red bean curd, with liquid (optional; see Note at left)*
- 2 tablespoons *hoisin sauce*
- 2 tablespoons *honey*
- 1 tablespoon plus 1 teaspoon *dark soy sauce*

Have butcher cut spareribs crosswise into 2-inch-wide strips. (You can do this yourself with a cleaver, but the butcher's band saw does a faster and cleaner job.) Marinate, roast, and baste as for Cantonese Roast Pork I (at left), but increase roasting time to 1 hour and 15 minutes. To serve, cut between bones into bite-sized pieces.

Serves 4 to 6 with other dishes.

HOW TO
AIR-DRY POULTRY

Thorough drying of the skin of both ducks and chickens is essential to roasting or smoking poultry Chinese style. Drying may be done after little or no preliminary cooking, but always precedes the final cooking. Hang the bird in a cool, airy place (out of reach of cats!) for at least 4 hours and up to 12 hours. Place a pan underneath the bird to catch drippings.

The easiest way to achieve a dry skin on a duck with the neck removed is to hang it by a loop of coat-hanger wire hooked through the flesh on both sides of the cavity.

A bird with the neck attached is easier to hang by a string looped around the neck approximately 6 inches away from the body. Use a chopstick to spread the wings, if present. After air-drying, refrigerate the bird for up to 24 hours.

CRISP-SKIN ROAST CHICKEN
Southern China

The Chinese do not roast chicken nearly as often as they do duck; simmering and steaming are usually preferred for the more delicate flesh of chicken. A large chicken can be roasted Chinese style with excellent results, however. This recipe uses the Cantonese technique of roasting with a liquid marinade inside the bird.

> 1 roasting chicken, 5 to 6 lbs
> ¼ cup dark soy sauce
> 2 tablespoons Shaoxing wine
> or dry sherry
> 1 teaspoon five-spice powder
> 2 green onions, halved
> 5 slices ginger
> Sichuan Pepper Salt (optional;
> see page 34)

1. Wash chicken thoroughly inside and out; pat dry with paper towels. Combine soy sauce, wine, five-spice powder, green onions, and ginger. Rub one third of this mixture over skin and inside of chicken. Hang to air-dry 6 to 12 hours. (See How to Air-Dry Poultry, at left.) Refrigerate remaining marinade.

2. Preheat oven to 400° F. Pour half remaining marinade inside chicken, and skewer or sew up opening. Place breast side up on a rack in a foil-lined roasting pan. Roast 15 minutes. Reduce heat to 350° F, and roast to an internal temperature of 150° F, a total cooking time of about 20 minutes per pound. Baste skin occasionally with reserved marinade during roasting.

3. Transfer chicken to a cutting board. Carefully remove thread or skewers and pour juices from cavity, along with any pan drippings, into a bowl. Carve chicken Chinese or Western style (see page 19), and arrange on a platter. Skim fat from reserved juices and serve as a dipping sauce, or serve chicken with Sichuan Pepper Salt.

Serves 4 to 6 with other dishes.

CRISP-SKIN ROAST DUCK
Northern China

This is a home version of the famous Peking Duck. The process may seem involved, but much of the preparation takes place a day or two ahead of roasting. Each of the steps is essential to produce a crisp skin and a relatively fat-free duck. Thorough drying of the skin is especially important, so don't skimp on the drying time. A vertical poultry roaster is definitely not traditional Chinese equipment, but it does a good job of simulating the traditional method of roasting the ducks hanging from the roof of the oven.

> 1 duck (preferably fresh),
> 4 to 5 lbs
> ½ cup water
> 1 tablespoon dark soy sauce
> 2 tablespoons honey or brown
> sugar
> Mandarin Pancakes (see
> page 114) or Flower Rolls
> (see page 113)
> Duck Sauce I, II, or III
> (see page 36)

1. Wash duck thoroughly inside and out. Remove head and feet, if present; cut off wings at first joint; remove neck, if desired. Massage skin all over to loosen it from meat. Where possible, slip fingers between skin and meat to loosen skin further.

2. Secure a loop of kitchen twine around the bird's neck, or hook a loop of wire through it. (Instructions for doing this and for hanging the bird to air-dry are in How to Air-Dry Poultry, at left.) In a wok or other large pan, bring at least 8 cups water to a boil. Holding duck by string or wire, lower it as far as possible into water. Ladle boiling water over exposed parts of duck. Cook 5 minutes, turning duck frequently and ladling water over exposed skin constantly. Remove duck from water and hang to dry over a drip pan in a cool, airy spot. Reserve water and duck trimmings for stock, if desired.

3. In a small saucepan heat the ½ cup water; stir in soy sauce and honey. Using basting brush, paint duck with mixture, allow to dry 15 minutes, paint again, and allow to dry again; continue for up to 5 coats.

4. Let duck dry 6 to 12 hours. An electric fan will speed drying. Duck may be roasted after drying or stored up to 2 days in refrigerator. If refrigerated, remove and hang again to dry for several more hours before roasting.

5. Preheat oven to 500° F. Place duck on a vertical poultry roaster over a foil-lined roasting pan. Place pan on lowest rack in oven, or on 2 shelves laid one on top if the other on oven floor. Loosely cover top of bird with a tent of foil. Roast 10 minutes. Reduce heat to 350° F, remove foil, and roast until skin is crisp and brown, 45 minutes longer. With a bulb baster, remove fat from roasting pan every 15 minutes during roasting. Rotate rack, if necessary, to brown duck completely.

6. Carve duck in kitchen or table, cutting meat into thin strips with skin attached. Serve with Mandarin Pancakes or Flower Rolls and one of the Duck Sauces.

Serves 4 to 8 with other dishes.

<u>Note</u> If using a regular roasting rack, start bird breast side up and do not cover with foil. Turn bird breast side down after first 10 minutes, roast 20 minutes, and return breast side up for last 25 minutes.

Air-drying followed by roasting Cantonese style with an internal marinade gives Crisp-Skin Roast Chicken a delightful combination of crackling skin and tender, moist meat.

Chinese cooks do not hesitate to combine several cooking methods for better results. Simmered Roast Duck is a perfect example; simmering or roasting alone would not produce the same effect.

SIMMERED ROAST DUCK
Eastern China

Chinese recipes often combine two cooking methods. In this case, simmering the duck first in a soy sauce mixture, called a master sauce, adds flavor, removes some of the fat, and partially cooks the duck, which cuts down on the roasting time. Incidentally, the watercress garnish is not just for looks; its sharp, peppery flavor complements the rich, slightly sweet duck.

> *Master sauce from Red-Cooked Chicken (see page 77)*
> 1 *green onion, sliced (optional; see step 1)*
> 2 *star anise pods (optional; see step 1)*
> ½ *cinnamon stick, crumbled (optional; see step 1)*
> *2-inch strip dried orange peel (optional; see step 1)*
> 1 *duck, 4 to 5 lbs*
> 1 *bunch watercress, washed and dried*
> *Sichuan Pepper Salt (see page 34) or a soy-based dipping sauce (see page 36)*

1. In a wok or other large, deep pan, bring master sauce to a boil. If using a reserved master sauce, add the green onion, star anise, cinnamon, and orange peel to reinforce the flavor. If making the sauce from scratch, simply follow the recipe on page 77.

2. Meanwhile, wash duck thoroughly inside and out; pat dry with paper towels. Remove feet, if present, cut off wings at first joint, and remove neck and head, if desired. These parts can be saved for stock. Prick skin several times around thighs and base of neck with a sharp-tined fork or skewer.

3. Slide duck into boiling sauce, breast side up. While liquid returns to a boil, continuously ladle sauce over exposed parts of duck. Reduce heat, cover, and simmer 15 minutes, basting occasionally. Turn duck over and simmer 15 minutes more, then turn off heat and let duck steep 30 minutes to 1 hour.

4. Remove duck from master sauce and drain thoroughly. Hang duck to dry in a cool, airy spot for 2 to 12 hours (see How to Air-Dry Poultry, page 88). (Drying is optional but gives the duck a crisper skin.) Strain sauce through a fine strainer and refrigerate or freeze.

5. Preheat oven to 400° F. Roast duck on a rack, breast side up, until skin is deep brown and meat reaches an internal temperature of 150° F, about 45 minutes. Cut into pieces Chinese style, or carve Western style. Serve on a platter garnished with sprigs of watercress. Serve with Sichuan Pepper Salt or, if you prefer a liquid sauce, prepare one of the soy-based dipping sauces.

Serves 4 to 6 with other dishes.

BURIED COOKING

Cooking food encased in a hot, solid medium—sand, clay, embers, or salt, for example—gives a slow roasting effect. The best-known example of this technique is the famous "Beggar's Chicken," which is wrapped in leaves and then encased in a thick layer of clay for cooking. Legend has it that a tramp camping on a riverbank was preparing to cook a stolen chicken when he heard someone approaching. Fearful of being caught, he quickly covered the chicken with mud, hid it in his fire, and ran away. When he returned, he broke open the clay to find a delicious, succulent chicken. A much less troublesome version of "buried" cooking follows.

SALT-BURIED CHICKEN
Southern China (Hakka)

This traditional Hakka dish is often called salt-baked chicken. A whole chicken is embedded in hot salt and cooked. As long as the skin is completely dry before cooking and the cavity is tightly closed to prevent leakage, the dish does not come out tasting salty. The chicken can be either baked in a 350° F oven for 1¼ hours or cooked on top of the stove, as described here.

> 1 chicken, 3 to 4 pounds
> 1 tablespoon Shaoxing wine or dry sherry
> 1 green onion, cut into 2-inch lengths
> 4 or 5 slices ginger
> Dried orange peel, 1 inch square (optional)
> 3 to 5 pounds kosher salt or other coarse salt
> Soy sauce, sesame oil, chile oil, and black vinegar, for dipping, or one or more dipping sauces (see page 36)

1. Wash chicken thoroughly inside and out; pat dry with paper towels. Rub wine over skin and set chicken on a rack. Allow to air-dry thoroughly, at least 4 hours at cool room temperature or overnight in the refrigerator. Remove from refrigerator at least 2 hours before cooking and hang up to finish drying. (See How to Air-Dry Poultry, page 88.)

2. Place green onion, ginger, and orange peel (if used) inside cavity. Truss chicken with kitchen twine. Wrap chicken in a single layer of cheesecloth, twisting ends together and tying near tail and neck with long loops of string.

3. In a wok or heavy casserole just large enough to hold chicken, heat salt over medium-high heat. When hot, transfer all but a 1-inch layer on bottom to another pan or a heatproof bowl. Set chicken in wok or casserole, breast side up, and cover with remaining hot salt. Cover, reduce heat to low, and cook until juices run clear, 1¼ hours.

4. Lift and brush salt from top of chicken. Lift chicken out of pot by the strings and transfer to a platter. Brush off remaining salt, and remove cheesecloth and trussing strings. Discard seasonings from cavity. Serve hot, warm, or cool, cut into pieces Chinese style or carved Western style (see page 19). Set table with individual bowls for each diner to make a dipping sauce, blending soy sauce, oils, and vinegar to taste, or serve a dipping sauce.

Serves 4 to 6 with other dishes.

Chicken buried in salt, Hakka style, and then cooked is incomparably tender and juicy—but, surprisingly, not salty.

SOUTHERN CHINA

The Chinese dishes that are familiar to Americans are mainly southern Chinese or Cantonese style. Most of the Chinese who emigrated during the late nineteenth and early twentieth centuries came from the southern provinces, particularly the areas around Guangzhou (Canton).

Southern China is rich in food resources. The subtropical climate and abundant rainfall make the region one of the most productive in China. Rice, sugar cane, tropical fruits, and many kinds of vegetables are grown there, and the sea provides fish and shellfish. The cuisine features the natural flavors of the fresh ingredients; the use of condiments and seasonings is more restrained. Southern cooks especially value texture. Stir-frying and steaming are the favorite cooking methods.

Southern Chinese cooking can be classified into several distinct styles. Classic Cantonese dishes include whole steamed fish with either a clear sauce or a more substantial black bean sauce; stir-fried lobster; meats cooked in oyster sauce, and "barbecued" pork. Canton is also the home of teahouses and those little delightful brunch foods known as dim sum (see page 115).

The city of Shantou is home for many Chinese who then emigrated to all parts of Southeast Asia; their cuisine, known as *chiu chow* or *teochiu,* is delicate and uses less oil than other southern cooking.

The third major southern cooking style is that of the Hakka, or "guest people," a northerly people who settled in the southeast hundreds of years ago. Hakka cooking is a blending of southern techniques and northern flavors (which includes a heavier use of garlic, onions, and wine). Salt-Buried Chicken (see page 91) is a Hakka specialty.

STOVE-TOP SMOKING

Smoking, Chinese style, unlike Western smoking, is not used to preserve foods, but for adding a smoky flavor to food before or after cooking by another method.

The Chinese have developed a unique method of stove-top smoking in a wok or other large, enclosed pan. (see Smoking in a Wok, page 95). The source of the smoke may be any combination of sugar, uncooked rice, tea leaves (especially scented teas such as jasmine or litchi), spices, and chips of aromatic camphor wood. This "fuel" is placed on the bottom of the pan, and the food to be smoked rests on a rack above it. The pan is covered and heated, and as the mixture burns it releases the flavoring smoke. Line the pan with foil for easier cleanup.

Smoked foods require several steps, but these can be done at your convenience. Tea-Smoked Duck, for example, needs a minimum of 12 hours to marinate, but can wait several days before steaming and smoking. The steaming and smoking steps can also be done ahead, leaving only the frying for the last minute.

TEA-SMOKED DUCK
Southwestern China

Smoked duck is a Sichuan specialty, a variation of the equally famous Fragrant Crunchy Duck (see page 58). Steaming the duck cooks the meat and renders most of the fat beneath the skin. Smoking adds another dimension of flavor, and the final deep-frying crisps the skin.

> *1 duck (preferably fresh),*
> *4 to 5 lbs*
> *2 tablespoons Sichuan*
> *peppercorns*
> *3 tablespoons kosher salt*
> *2 green onions, cut into*
> *2-inch lengths*
> *4 or 5 slices ginger*
> *⅓ cup each tea leaves, brown*
> *sugar, and raw rice*
> *Oil, for deep-frying*
> *Flower Rolls (see page 113)*
> *or Plain Steamed Buns*
> *(see page 111)*

1. Wash duck thoroughly inside and out; pat dry with paper towels. Remove head and feet, if present; cut off wings at first joint; remove neck, if desired. Save these parts for stock.

2. Combine peppercorns and salt in a small skillet (preferably one with a nonstick surface) and place over medium heat. Cook, stirring or shaking pan frequently, until very fragrant, 3 to 5 minutes. Transfer mixture to a blender, spice grinder, food processor, or mortar; grind coarsely. Rub entire mixture all over skin and inside of duck. Place duck in a deep plate and marinate in refrigerator overnight or up to 3 days, turning a few times a day to marinate evenly.

3. Remove duck from refrigerator at least 1 hour before steaming. Drain off accumulated juices. Place green onion and ginger inside cavity. Steam duck in its plate 1½ hours (see Steaming, page 78). With a bulb baster, remove juices and fat from pan every 20 to 30 minutes. Drain duck thoroughly (it will have rendered over a cup of fat and juices). If desired, reserve juices for another use.

4. Combine tea, sugar, and rice. Following the instructions given in Smoking in a Wok, page 95, arrange mixture in an even layer on bottom of foil-lined wok. Smoke duck, breast side up, on rack for 15 minutes. Turn off heat and let stand 5 minutes more. Remove duck from wok and discard foil.

5. In a wok or other large, deep pan, heat about 6 cups oil to 375° F. Holding duck with a large Chinese wire skimmer, lower into oil and fry until crisp, about 10 minutes. Ladle oil over exposed parts and turn once during frying. If you prefer extra crispness, remove duck from oil, increase temperature to 400° F, and fry again briefly.

6. To serve, cut into pieces Chinese style (see page 20), or place on table whole, letting diners pull pieces from bird with chopsticks. Serve with Flower Rolls or Plain Steamed Buns, folding a bit of skin and meat into a piece of bread, like a sandwich.

Serves 6 to 8 with other dishes.

The triumph of Chinese-style
smoking is Tea-Smoked Duck, in
which the smoky aroma of
tea and rice mingle with the spicy
flavors of the marinade.

SMOKED TROUT

Any moderately rich fish can be smoked by this technique, and steaks or slices can be used in place of a whole fish. Although this is not really a preserving method, as is Western-style smoking, the smoked fish will keep several days in the refrigerator.

- 3 trout or pan-sized coho salmon, 8 to 10 oz each
- ¼ cup soy sauce
- 2 tablespoons Shaoxing wine or dry sherry
- 2 green onions, shredded
- 6 slices ginger
- 1 tablespoon kosher salt
- ½ teaspoon sugar
- ¼ cup each *tea leaves, brown sugar, and uncooked rice*
- 2 tablespoons Sichuan peppercorns
- 2 star anise pods, broken into points

1. Clean fish thoroughly, removing any trace of entrails from cavity. Rinse inside and out. In a shallow bowl, combine soy sauce, wine, green onion, ginger, salt, and sugar; marinate fish in this mixture 12 to 24 hours in the refrigerator. Turn fish in marinade and rub marinade into cavity every few hours.

2. Remove fish from marinade and steam 10 minutes on a plate (see Steaming, page 78).

3. Combine tea, sugar, rice, peppercorns, and star anise. Following instructions given in Smoking In a Wok, opposite page, arrange mixture in an even layer in bottom of foil-lined wok. Smoke fish on an oiled rack for 10 minutes. Turn off heat and let stand 10 minutes more. Serve hot, warm, or cold.

Serves 6 to 8 as an appetizer.

SMOKED CHICKEN WITH ORANGE PEEL
Southwestern China

Dried orange peel (see page 28) gives a special aroma to this smoked chicken. Served hot, warm, or cold, smoked chicken is a versatile meat that can be used in salads, noodle dishes, soups, fried rice, or anywhere you might use ham. It tastes even better a day or two after smoking, making it ideal for picnics.

> 1 chicken, 3 to 4 pounds
> Dried orange peel, 3 inches square, finely minced
> 3 tablespoons Sichuan Pepper Salt (see page 34)
> 2 green onions, cut into thirds
> 4 slices ginger
> ¼ cup each tea leaves, brown sugar, and uncooked rice
> 1 cinnamon stick, crumbled
> 1 pod star anise, broken into points

1. Wash chicken thoroughly inside and out; pat dry with paper towels. Combine orange peel and pepper salt; rub mixture all over skin and inside of chicken. Marinate in refrigerator up to 24 hours, turning occasionally.

2. Discard any juices that have accumulated, and place bird in a deep, heatproof plate or pie pan. Place green onion and ginger in cavity. Steam until juices show only a trace of pink, about 30 minutes (see Steaming, page 78). Remove juices with a bulb baster and reserve for another use. If chicken is not to be smoked immediately, refrigerate until 1 hour before smoking.

3. Combine tea, sugar, rice, cinnamon, and star anise. Following the instructions given in Smoking in a Wok, at right, arrange mixture in an even layer over bottom of foil-lined wok. Smoke chicken on an oiled rack for 15 minutes. Turn off heat and let stand 5 minutes more before serving.

Serves 6 to 8 with other dishes.

Variation Use 2 pounds chicken legs or wings in place of a whole chicken. Omit green onion and ginger, or add them to steaming plate. Reduce steaming time to 20 minutes.

Step-by-Step

SMOKING IN A WOK

Keep a window open or your kitchen fan going while practicing this cooking technique. Be sure to line both the top and bottom of your wok with foil and crimp it so that only a small stream of smoke escapes. Discard foil immediately after you've finished cooking to rid your kitchen of the smoky smell.

1. *Line inside of wok and lid with a 24-inch square of heavy-duty aluminum foil. Leave edges of foil loose. Arrange smoking ingredients specified in recipe in an even layer on bottom of pan.*

3. *Place pan over high heat until mixture begins to burn and release smoke. Reduce heat to medium, cover pan, and crimp edges of foil together, leaving only a small vent.*

4. *Adjust heat and foil so that smoke comes out of the vent in a thin stream. You will probably want to open a window or turn the kitchen vent fan on now to help eliminate smoky odors from your house.*

2. *Place food to be smoked on an oiled rack at least 1 inch above smoking mixture. A 10-inch-diameter round cake rack works well in a 14-inch wok.*

5. *After required smoking time, remove food. Immediately wrap up and discard foil.*

GRILLING

Grilling food directly over an open fire is not as common in China as in other parts of Asia. Restaurants in the south may offer such foreign grilled dishes as the Malay *satay* (thin strips of spiced meat grilled on skewers), and in the northwestern provinces along the old Silk Route, minced lamb is molded on skewers and grilled using a Middle Eastern technique. The most characteristically Chinese method of grilling, adopted from the nomadic peoples of the northwest, is the Mongolian-style barbecue. Restaurants featuring this style of cooking are popular in many parts of China, especially the northern cities.

Like hot-pot cooking, Mongolian-style barbecue is a do-it-yourself affair. Diners cooks their own thin slices of lamb or beef on a charcoal brazier in the middle of the table, dipping the slices into sauces blended to their liking. This style of eating makes a great informal meal. All that is needed is a hibachi or other small tabletop grill, chopsticks (long cooking chopsticks are handy), and small bowls to hold dipping sauces. In nice weather, grill outside over charcoal; in winter, however, use a grill that can be used indoors.

Caution Do not use a charcoal grill indoors. Burning charcoal gives off carbon monoxide gas, which can be dangerous or fatal if allowed to concentrate. Fortunately, there are portable grills fueled by bottled gas or with electric heating elements that do the job nicely.

The traditional accompaniments to a Mongolian-style barbecue are barley soup made from a lamb stock and grilled green onions. In northern restaurants the meal includes steamed bread or pancakes. Other soups and rice or noodles can certainly be substituted, and a vegetable side dish can be added if you like. Don't try to make a Mongolian barbecue part of a fancy multicourse meal, however; it really deserves center stage.

BARBECUED BEEF, BEIJING STYLE

Mongolian barbecue is very popular in Beijing, where this variation developed. Unmarinated slices of beef are grilled and immediately dipped into beaten egg. A thin layer of egg cooks onto the meat, which helps the sauces to cling. The best beef cuts for grilling are also best for stir-frying. See the list on page 32.

> 1   to 1½ pounds boneless
>   tender beef
> 4   to 6 eggs (1 per person)
> 12 green onions, trimmed and
>   cut into 2-inch lengths
>   Soy sauce, for dipping
>   Minced ginger, for dipping
>   Minced garlic, for dipping
>   Chile oil, sauce, or paste with
>   garlic, for dipping
>   Hot Mustard Sauce (see page
>   36), for dipping
>   Black or rice vinegar,
>   for dipping
>   Hoisin sauce, for dipping
>   Plain Steamed Buns (see page
>   111), Flower Rolls (see page
>   113), or Mandarin Pancakes
>   (see page 114)

1. Preheat grill. Slice beef thinly across grain into 1- by 3-inch pieces. (Partially frozen meat is easier to slice thinly.) Arrange on a serving dish with green onions in center.

2. Set a bowl with a beaten egg at each place, and another for dipping sauce. Pass sauces and condiments for each diner to mix a dipping sauce to taste. Each diner grills meat slices and green onions until done to taste, turning and retrieving with chopsticks. (Allow 15 seconds to 1 minute per side, according to taste and heat of fire.) As soon as a slice is cooked, dip immediately and briefly into egg and then into dipping sauce. Fold into a Plain Steamed Bun, Flower Roll, or Mandarin Pancake, and eat it like a sandwich.

Serves 4 to 6.

Hot off the grill, bites of
Barbecued Beef, Beijing Style, are
dipped in raw egg and then
into a dipping sauce assembled to
taste from assorted condiments.

An unorthodox, but delicious, combination features Mongolian lamb, Korean kim chee, Middle Eastern pilaf, Chinese braised vegetables, and California wine.

MONGOLIAN BARBECUE

*Mongolian
Barbecued Lamb*

Bulgur Pilaf

*Braised Assorted Vegetables
(see page 74)*

Perfect for casual entertaining or a family meal, this dinner combines traditional Chinese elements and foreign influences. Bulgur wheat is a delicious (but thoroughly un-Chinese) accompaniment to catch the dripping juices of the lamb.

Kim chee, or pickled cabbage, is a Korean side dish that marries well with these dishes. It can be found in the refrigerated section of Korean markets, and increasingly in super-markets. Serve a full-flavored red wine, such as a California Zinfandel or a French Côtes-du-Rhône. This menu serves 4 to 6 diners.

MONGOLIAN BARBECUED LAMB

   1   *to 1½ pounds boneless leg
         of lamb*
   4   *lamb kidneys (optional)*
  12   *green onions, trimmed and
         cut into 2-inch lengths
         Soy sauce, for dipping
         Minced ginger, for dipping
         Minced garlic, for dipping
         Chile oil, sauce, or paste with
         garlic, for dipping
         Hot Mustard Sauce (see page
         36), for dipping
         Black or rice vinegar, for
         dipping*

1. Separate lamb into individual muscles along natural seams and remove tough membranes. Slice across grain into thin pieces, about 1 inch by 3 inches. (Partially frozen meat is easier to slice thinly.) Split kidneys (if used) in half lengthwise, and remove any tubes and gristle. Slice thinly. Arrange sliced meats in an attractive pattern on one or more serving platters. Pile green onions in center of platter.

2. Oil grill and preheat thoroughly. (If using charcoal, allow fire to burn until coals are covered with light gray ash but are still quite hot.) Place grill on a fireproof trivet or other heatproof base in center of table, within reach of all diners.

3. Pass sauces and condiments for each diner to mix a dipping sauce to taste. Each diner grills slices of meat to taste, turning and retrieving with chopsticks. (Allow 15 seconds to 1 minute per side according to taste and heat of fire.) Dip meat into sauce before eating. Grill green onion pieces alongside meat until lightly browned and soft, 1 to 2 minutes.

Variation Slices of meat may be marinated before grilling, instead of or in addition to dipping in sauce after cooking. You may wish to set two bowls at each place—a larger one for the marinade and a smaller one for the dipping sauce. Soy sauce, ginger, and garlic make a good marinating mixture, while stronger flavors like mustard and chile paste go better in the dipping sauce.

BULGUR PILAF

Bulgur (coarse cracked wheat) is not used in China, but it is common in the Middle East. Strange as it might seem to traditional Chinese tastes, it makes a good accompaniment to grilled lamb in any culture. It can also stand in for rice or noodles in any northern Chinese menu.

   2   *tablespoons oil*
   1   *tablespoon minced shallot
         or green onion*
  1½   *cups bulgur wheat*
   3   *cups Basic Chicken Stock
         (see page 64)*
   ½   *teaspoon kosher salt*

In a heavy saucepan heat oil over medium heat. Sauté shallot until fragrant but not browned. Stir in bulgur and cook until surface of grains changes color slightly, about 3 minutes. Add stock and salt; bring to a boil. Cover, reduce heat, and simmer until liquid is absorbed, about 30 minutes.

Rice, in the form of grains, noodles, or flour, is a major food staple. Together with wheat and other grains, it provides most of the calories in the Chinese diet.

Rice, Noodles, Breads & "Little Dishes"

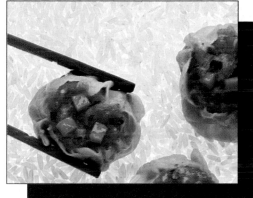

Cereal foods are the most important part of the Chinese diet. The "daily bread" of the Chinese may be rice, noodles, or steamed or pan-fried bread. Rice is served at nearly every meal in southern China and is also served in other regions of the country. Wheat-flour breads are the great staple of the North, but they too have spread to other regions. Noodles are a favorite food all over China. And both noodle and bread doughs form the wrappers for those delightful little tidbits known as dim sum.

RICE

So far, the recipes in this book have been for what the Chinese call *tsai*, or dishes. Another important part of the Chinese diet is *fan*, or grain foods. Rice, wheat flour, and, to a lesser extent, other grains provide most of the calories in the Chinese diet, in the form of carbohydrates. They also provide a bland flavor background for more highly seasoned foods.

A perfect bowl of Chinese rice consists of grains that are tender but not soft, with just enough sticky coating on the grains to make them easy to eat with chopsticks.

RICE VARIETIES

The hundreds of varieties of rice grown in Asia can be loosely grouped into three categories, according to their cooking characteristics: long grain, short grain, and glutinous. Beside the obvious difference in shape, the rice varieties differ in the composition of the starches in the grain. This determines how the grains swell in cooking and how much they stick together.

Long-grain rice is the type most familiar to Americans and favored by many Chinese. It is the least "sticky" variety, cooking into a fluffy bowl of firm, separate grains. Most of the rice grown in the southern United States is of this type. Do not use parboiled ("converted") rice for Chinese-style cooking unless you plan to eat with a fork; otherwise, you will be picking up one grain of rice at a time with your chopsticks.

Short-grain rice is the type favored by most Japanese and many Chinese. The grains have a more oval shape and cook up softer and stickier than long-grain rice, with a slightly fuller and sweeter flavor. Some cooks distinguish between the true short-grain rices, such as pearl rice, and the medium-grain varieties such as Calrose and various others with the word "rose" in the name. Both types are widely grown in California, primarily for the Asian market. The medium-grain types offer the best compromise between firm and soft, separate and sticky. Shorter varieties require less water for cooking than long-grain rice.

Glutinous rice is a special category of short-grain rice, also known as "sweet" or "sticky" rice. True to its name, it cooks to the softest and stickiest consistency of all (but the taste is not noticeably sweeter than other rice). Glutinous rice is typically steamed rather than boiled, for use in stuffings (see Eight-Treasure Duck, page 57) or for a special sweet rice pudding served at banquets. It is not interchangeable with other short-grain varieties.

Brown rice, while nutritionally superior to white rice, is not popular with the Chinese. White rice is more easily digestible, especially in the quantities consumed by rice-eating Chinese. However, if you prefer, you can certainly serve it with your Chinese meals. Brown rice is available in long-, medium-, and short-grain varieties.

COOKING RICE

Chinese-style rice is either boiled or steamed. What is typically called "steamed rice" in restaurants is in fact cooked by the absorption method, described in Basic 'Steamed' Rice (see opposite page). True steamed rice takes longer to cook, and the absorption method is nearly foolproof.

The instructions for the absorption method are approximate. The rice may require more or less water, depending on the shape of the pot (deep or shallow), the exact strain of rice you are using, and even the age of the rice (new-crop rice takes less water; older rice more). The amount also makes a difference; twice as much rice does not mean twice as much water. Ultimately, it is a matter of taste and experience. If you prefer a more scientific form of measurement, use the following rule: For long-grain rice, use 2 cups water for the first cup of rice and 1 cup water per additional cup; for medium- or short-grain rice, use 1½ cups water for the first cup and 1 cup water per additional cup.

An electric rice cooker is a common feature in many Chinese kitchens. These appliances cook rice to a perfect consistency every time, and they free a stove burner for other uses. If you cook a lot of Asian-style meals, an electric cooker is a handy item to have. Follow manufacturer's instructions.

Chinese-style rice is never salted. For one thing, many of the dishes served with the rice contain plenty of salt. While Westerners may find unsalted rice extremely bland, to the Chinese the very blandness of rice is a virtue: It does not add to or subtract from the accompanying dishes, but just serves as a background. Still, if you prefer, you can add salt to your rice, but decrease the salt in other dishes accordingly.

Chinese cooks always wash rice thoroughly before cooking, to remove excess starch (see "Basic 'Steamed' Rice," steps 1 and 2). Most rice comes from the mill with a light dusting of starch to absorb moisture and keep the grains fresh. Most rice packages say that washing is not necessary, and doing so clearly washes away some of the nutrients in the rice; however, finicky rice cooks insist on washing it anyway, saying it gives the rice a "cleaner" taste. Try it both ways and decide for yourself.

Leftover rice can be reheated by steaming, made into Rice Porridge (see page 104), or used for Sizzling Rice Cakes (see page 104) or any of the recipes for fried rice (see pages 103–105).

FRIED RICE WITH HAM, EGG, AND CABBAGE

What started as a way to use leftover rice has become a quite popular dish in its own right—fried rice. Actually, the name is a bit of a misnomer; the rice is not really fried, but stir-fried in a little oil along with bits of meat and vegetables. The catchall version found in some restaurants, dark brown with soy sauce, does not compare to good homemade fried rice with a couple of carefully chosen ingredients. Season fried rice dishes with salt, not soy sauce, to preserve the color of the rice.

- 2 to 3 tablespoons oil
- 1 egg, beaten
- 1 teaspoon minced ginger
- 1 clove garlic, minced
- ⅓ pound bok choy, cut crosswise into ¼-inch slices
- 1½ ounces (trimmed) Smithfield ham, soaked in water 30 minutes, drained, and thinly sliced
- 2 tablespoons cloud ears, soaked until soft and drained
- 2 to 3 cups cooked rice, at room temperature
  Salt, to taste
- ¼ cup Basic Chicken Stock (see page 64)

1. Heat wok or skillet over medium-high heat, and add 1 tablespoon of the oil. Pour beaten egg into pan and swirl to make a large, flat omelet. Cook egg just until set, transfer to cutting board, and cut into thin 1-inch strips.

2. Add remaining oil to pan. Add ginger and garlic; cook until fragrant. Add bok choy, ham, and cloud ears; stir-fry until heated through, about 2 minutes.

3. Add rice to pan and stir to break up clumps. Stir-fry vigorously, scraping up any bits of rice that cling to pan. When rice begins to brown, add salt to taste (allow for saltiness of ham), then add stock and egg strips. Turn heat to high and stir-fry until liquid is nearly all evaporated. Transfer to serving platter.

Serves 2 as a one-dish meal, 4 or more with other dishes.

Step-by-Step

BASIC "STEAMED" RICE

What is commonly known as "steamed" rice is actually cooked by the absorption method. This technique works for any type of rice, but the ratio of water to rice will differ. In a typical meal, allow ⅓ to ⅔ cup uncooked rice per person.

Basic rice-to-water ratios are:
  Long-grain rice—2 cups water for first cup of rice; 1 cup water for each additional cup of rice.
  Medium- and short-grain rice— 1½ cups water for first cup of rice; 1 cup of water for each additional cup of rice.

1. *Measure rice into bowl or cooking pot. Cover with cold water. Swirl with your hand several times until water becomes cloudy. Pour out water (use a hand-held strainer to catch any grains that pour out with the water).*

3. *Bring to a boil, cover, reduce heat, and simmer until water is absorbed, about 15 minutes for short- or medium-grain rice. Lift cover only long enough to check that rice has absorbed water, then cover again. Turn off heat and let stand 10 minutes longer. Fluff with a fork or chopsticks before serving.*

2. *Repeat washing procedure until water is clear, 3 to 5 times in all. Drain rice thoroughly and transfer to cooking pot. Cover with cold water 1 inch deeper than depth of rice. Many cooks use one joint of a finger or thumb as a measure.*

Glutinous rice is steamed by a different method. After soaking the rice in cold water for several hours, spread it in a thin layer in a bamboo or metal steamer lined with cheesecloth. Steam until rice is tender, about 25 minutes.

SIZZLING RICE CAKES

Flat cakes of rice, deep-fried until crisp and then rushed to the table, give a delightful sizzling sound when combined with hot liquids. Sizzling Rice Soup (see page 66) is the best-known example, but a saucy stir-fry poured over the cakes produces the same effect. In restaurants, sizzling rice is typically made from the layer of rice that sticks to the pot and gets slightly scorched. Leftover boiled rice can also be pressed into cakes and fried, or you can use the following method of cooking rice just for this purpose.

> 1 cup uncooked rice (long or short grain)
> 2 cups water (approximately)
> 1 to 2 tablespoons oil
> Oil, for deep-frying

1. Wash rice (if using a short-grain variety) and place in a 10-inch skillet or other shallow pan with a tight-fitting cover. Add water to cover by almost an inch. Cover, bring to a boil, reduce to a simmer, and cook 30 minutes over a very low flame or in a low oven. Remove cover and check to see that all the water has been absorbed. If not, cover and cook a little longer. Do not stir rice.

2. When rice is done, drizzle entire surface with oil. Let oil seep under rice, then loosen from pan with a spatula. Cut into cakes that are about 2 by 3 inches.

3. Pour oil into a skillet to a depth of ½ inch. Heat until a grain of rice added to oil sizzles rapidly. Fry rice cakes until light golden. If necessary, fry cakes in batches, but return first batch to oil for a final crisping just before serving. Drain only briefly (some hot oil should cling to the cakes), and serve immediately.

Makes about 8 rice cakes.

RICE PORRIDGE WITH ASSORTED TOPPINGS
Southern China

Known as *congee* to the English-speaking residents of Asia and as *jook* in Cantonese, this soupy form of rice is the traditional southern Chinese breakfast. It is also popular as a late-night snack, and in most any China-town you will find a few restaurants open until the wee hours serving jook. By itself, it is unbelievably bland, and so it is always served with salty additions such as pickled vegetables, sausage, salt-preserved eggs, or leftover meats liberally seasoned with soy sauce. Some suggested toppings follow.

> ¼ cup uncooked rice
> 3 cups water

Wash rice and place in a heavy, covered pan. Add water, bring to a boil, cover, and reduce heat to the lowest possible setting. Simmer, stirring occasionally, until rice is very soft and liquid thickens, about 2 hours. Add one of the following toppings and cook just long enough to heat toppings, then serve in deep bowls with additional salt or soy sauce to taste.

Serves 2.

<u>Note</u> Jook can also be made with leftover cooked rice; just add water and simmer until very tender. Whether using raw or cooked rice, the amount of water may be varied to produce a thinner or thicker porridge.

Toppings

☐ Add sliced leftover Red-Cooked Pork Shoulder (see page 69) with some of its master sauce and sliced green onions.

☐ Add sliced hard-cooked eggs, well salted, and sliced Chinese sausage, steamed in a bowl to rid it of excess fat. (Salt-preserved eggs, sold in Chinese markets, are more authentic; they can be hard-cooked just like fresh eggs. The yolks have a striking orange color.)

☐ Add poached egg and preserved Sichuan mustard greens, rinsed and sliced.

☐ Add cooked and shredded chicken and black mushroom caps that have been soaked and sliced.

SHRIMP AND MUSHROOM FRIED RICE

Here is one case where canned water chestnuts are actually preferable to fresh; the fresh variety is so sweet that it would upset the balance of this delicately flavored dish. This fried rice is also more typical of restaurant versions, being flavored and colored with soy sauce.

> Oil, for stir-frying
> 1 tablespoon minced ginger
> 2 green onions, cut into 1½-inch lengths
> ¼ pound small shrimp, peeled and split lengthwise
> 3 dried black mushroom caps, soaked and drained and cut into strips (reserve soaking liquid)
> ¼ cup sliced canned water chestnuts
> ¼ cup fresh or frozen peas
> 2 to 3 cups cooked rice, at room temperature
> 1 tablespoon soy sauce
> Fresh coriander sprigs, for garnish (optional)

1. Heat wok over medium-high heat, and add oil. Add ginger and cook until fragrant. Add green onions, shrimp, mushrooms, and water chestnuts; stir-fry until heated through.

2. Add peas and rice; stir-fry, scraping pan thoroughly. Add soy sauce and 3 tablespoons of the reserved mushroom-soaking water; cook until nearly dry. Transfer to serving platter, and garnish with coriander, if desired.

Serves 2 as a one-dish meal, 4 or more with other dishes.

SAUSAGE AND FENNEL FRIED RICE

Fresh fennel, also known as sweet anise, is not a typical Chinese vegetable, but its sweet, licorice-tinged flavor and crunchy texture are perfectly at home in a Chinese dish. It combines beautifully with the sweet-spicy Cantonese sausage, *lop cheong*. Bok choy provides a refreshing note of bitterness.

    2   Chinese sausages
    ¼   cup oil
    ¼   cup raw peanuts, preferably
        with red skins
    1   teaspoon each *minced ginger
        and garlic*
    1   cup sliced bok choy, preferably
        the green-stemmed variety
    1   small fennel bulb, trimmed,
        split lengthwise, and cut cross-
        wise into ¼-inch slices
    2 to 3 cups cooked rice, at
        room temperature
    ¼   cup Basic Chicken Stock (see
        page 64)
        Salt, to taste

1. Slice sausages thinly on the diagonal. Steam in a bowl for 10 minutes to render some of the fat. Drain and discard fat. (This may be done ahead of time.)

2. Heat wok or skillet over medium heat, and add oil. Fry peanuts until light brown. Remove and drain on paper towels.

3. Remove all but 2 tablespoons oil from pan. Add ginger and garlic; cook until fragrant. Add sausage and bok choy; stir-fry 1 minute. Add fennel and cook 30 seconds more. Add rice and stir-fry, scraping pan thoroughly, until lightly browned. Add stock and salt and cook until nearly dry. Transfer to serving platter and scatter peanuts over top.

Serves 2 as a one-dish meal, 4 or more with other dishes.

Fried rice lends itself to all sorts of variations; this version combines Chinese sausage and cabbage with fresh fennel, a vegetable of Mediterranean origin. Use your imagination to create other new combinations.

An assortment of Chinese noodles and dumpling wrappers. On tray: dried egg noodles of various shapes; clockwise from upper right: bean threads, two sizes of dried wheat-flour noodles, precooked rice noodles, and fresh wrappers—square for wontons and round for siu mai or potstickers.

NOODLES

Noodles have been an important part of the Chinese diet since the Han dynasty period (206 B.C. to A.D. 220), when the Chinese learned flour-milling technology from an unknown neighbor to the west. Before this time, most grains were simply boiled whole, as rice is today; but finely milled flour could be combined with water, kneaded and worked into various shapes, and cooked by various methods to produce noodles, dumplings, and breads.

Made with or without egg, of wheat flour, rice flour, or bean starch, noodles (*mein*) remain one of the most popular of Chinese foods. They are served hot or cold, boiled, stir-fried, deep-fried, or simmered in soup. Noodle doughs form the wrappers for all sorts of Chinese dumplings and savory pastries (see Dim Sum, page 115).

If you live near a Chinatown, you should be able to get all sorts of fresh Chinese-style noodles and wrappers. Well-stocked supermarkets also carry them. Or, you can make Chinese Egg Noodle Dough (see opposite page).

TYPES OF NOODLES

Unless another type is specified, the noodle recipes in this book call for a very thin egg noodle, the kind sold in sealed plastic packages as "Chinese-style noodles" or "extrathin mein." They are square or rectangular in cross section, about 1/16 inch thick, and they correspond closely to home-made noodles cut on the narrowest cutter of a pasta machine. Dried vermicelli or thin Japanese *ramen* may be used as a substitute. If you prefer a thicker noodle, look for the type labeled "chow mein noodles," which are about as thick as spaghetti.

Rice-flour noodles are sold in several forms. Both narrow and wide noodles are sold dried, labeled "rice vermicelli" or "rice sticks." These generally do not need to be boiled, simply soaked in warm water until soft. They can be used in place of egg noodles in *chow mein* or *lo mein* dishes. Fresh rice noodles are sold in well-stocked Chinese markets in plastic-wrapped trays. Whole sheets of fresh rice noodle are used in some *dim sum* preparations, and the cut noodles may be briefly steamed to accompany red-cooked or braised meats or stir-fried dishes.

"Bean threads" is just one of the names for the most unusual type of Chinese noodle. Also known as cellophane noodles, glass noodles, pea-starch noodles, and Chinese vermicelli, these thin, transparent noodles are made from mung bean starch (the bean used to make bean sprouts). They are typically used in simmered or braised dishes (see Red-Braised Duck page 75 and Banquet Firepot, page 70) rather than in dry preparations. Like rice vermicelli, they do not need to be cooked, merely soaked until soft. Unlike other noodles, they can simmer along with braised meats for an hour or more without falling apart, all the time absorbing flavor. Bean threads can also be fried, without any preliminary soaking. Just a few seconds in hot oil turns them into crisp white sticks, good for garnishing other dishes or as a base for a salad.

BOILING NOODLES

Most Chinese noodle dishes call for the noodles to be boiled first and then either combined with a sauce or given some further treatment such as stir-frying. With homemade or packaged fresh noodles, fluff them a little first to loosen the clumps, and then drop them into a large pot of lightly salted water at a rolling boil. Stir immediately with long chopsticks or a spoon to separate the noodles, and begin tasting them as soon as the water returns to the boil; most will be done within a few seconds. Dried noodles take longer; follow the package directions. Drain cooked noodles in a colander in the sink and, unless you will be saucing them immediately, rinse with cold water to prevent further cooking. Toss the noodles under running water by hand so you can feel when they are thoroughly cooled. Drain well and toss with a little oil to keep them from sticking. If sufficiently oiled and tightly wrapped, noodles can be kept several hours or even overnight in the refrigerator.

CHINESE EGG NOODLE DOUGH

This dough can be used for Chinese-style noodles as well as for dumpling and spring-roll wrappers. Making your own noodle dough is a snap with an Italian-style pasta maker. It can also be made by hand with a rolling pin, although this technique takes a little practice.

1 large egg
2 tablespoons water
1 cup flour (approximately)
¼ cup cornstarch (approximately)

1. In a medium bowl combine egg and water; beat lightly with a fork or chopsticks. Stir in ¾ cup of the flour and mix until dough forms clumps.

2. Turn dough out onto a board dusted with remaining flour. Knead until smooth, kneading in remaining flour. Add additional flour only if necessary to keep dough from sticking. Invert bowl over dough and let rest for 15 to 30 minutes.

3. *To prepare with a pasta machine:* Scrape board clean and dust with some of the cornstarch. Divide dough into 2 or 4 pieces for easier handling, if desired. Set rollers at widest setting. Flatten a piece of dough by hand to about ¼ inch thickness, dust with cornstarch, and pass dough through rollers to form a thin oval. Fold each end over the middle, forming three layers. Dust outside again and roll. Repeat 4 or 5 times, until dough is smooth, stretchy, and pliable. Turn rollers to next smaller setting and roll out once (do not fold). Continue rolling, reducing thickness one setting with each roll, until dough is the desired thickness. If sheets of dough become too long to handle easily, cut in half and continue rolling with each piece.

To prepare by hand: Scrape board clean and dust with cornstarch. Divide dough in half and set one piece aside. Flatten other piece by hand to about ¼ inch thickness, then roll out into a large oval with a rolling pin. Dust dough with cornstarch as necessary to prevent sticking. Starting at one edge of dough, wrap a little dough around the pin and roll toward center, trapping a layer of dough between the pin and the rest of the dough. Roll pin back and forth several times with both palms against the pin, stretching the dough sideways along the pin. Roll another few inches of dough around the pin, and repeat the process. When you reach the middle of the sheet, unroll the dough, turn it around, and repeat from the other end. Roll finished sheet to reduce any thick spots.

4. Spread rolled sheets of dough out to dry on table, on clean towels, or drape them over a clean broomstick or the back of a chair. Allow to dry slightly, but not so much that they become brittle. Cut sheets into noodles of desired size with cutter attachment of pasta machine, or by rolling a sheet up from one end and cutting the roll into narrow coils.

Makes about ½ pound noodles.

STIR-FRIED NOODLES WITH SHREDDED PORK
Lo mein

This style of stir-frying noodles along with their toppings is sometimes called *chow mein*, but *lo mein* (mixed noodles) is more descriptive. It's hard to define where one method ends and the other begins, but lo mein is usually not cooked as brown or as crisp as chow mein.

> ½ pound thin Chinese-style egg noodles, boiled and drained
> 4 to 5 tablespoons oil
> ¼ cup Basic or Rich chicken stock (see page 64)
> 1 tablespoon dark soy sauce
> 1 teaspoon salt
> 1 tablespoon shredded ginger
> 2 green onions, cut into 1-inch lengths
> ½ cup shredded pork
> 2 or 3 large leaves bok choy or choy sum, cut into 2-inch slices

1. Toss noodles with 2 tablespoons of the oil to coat evenly. Set aside. (This may be done several hours ahead.) Combine stock, soy sauce, and salt; set aside.

2. Heat wok over medium-high heat, and add 1 tablespoon of the oil. Add ginger and green onion; cook until fragrant. Add pork shreds and stir-fry until meat starts to lose its raw color. Add bok choy and stir-fry 1 minute longer, then transfer mixture to a warm plate.

3. Wipe wok clean with a paper towel and add another tablespoon or two of the oil. Reduce heat to medium. Swirl wok to cover sides with oil, then add noodles. Cook without stirring 1 minute, then begin stirring and tossing noodles to brown them in places. Add a little more oil, if necessary, to keep noodles from sticking.

4. When noodles are heated through and lightly browned in places, add stock mixture and stir to loosen noodles from pan. Return pork mixture to pan and toss with noodles. Turn heat to high and continue cooking and stirring until liquid is nearly gone, then transfer to serving plate.

Serves 4 with other dishes.

MIXED SHELLFISH CHOW MEIN

Real *chow mein*, literally, pan-fried noodles, is a far cry from the Americanized version made with thick canned fried noodles. In the genuine article, noodles that have first been boiled and drained are cooked to order in a wok or skillet and then combined with a savory stir-fry of meat, seafood, or vegetables. The noodles may be stir-fried briefly, like a crisper version of *lo mein* or, as in the following recipe, formed into a loose, flat cake and pan-fried separately until the outside is browned but the inside is still soft. Any imaginable stir-fried dish can be served this way, as long as there is enough sauce to moisten the noodles.

> ½ pound thin Chinese-style egg noodles, boiled and drained
> 4 to 6 tablespoons oil
> ¼ cup Basic Chicken Stock (see page 64)
> 2 tablespoons soy sauce
> ½ teaspoon cornstarch
> 1 tablespoon minced ginger
> 2 green onions, sliced
>   Pinch red-pepper flakes (optional)
> ¼ to ½ pound shellfish:
>   Small or medium shrimp, peeled, deveined, and split lengthwise
>   Squid, cleaned and cut as described in Squid With Black Bean Sauce (see page 46)
>   Scallops, sliced in half if large
> ½ cup straw mushrooms
> 1 cup sliced baby bok choy or other tender greens

1. Toss noodles with 1 to 2 tablespoons oil to coat evenly. (This may be done several hours ahead.)

2. Combine stock, soy sauce, and cornstarch; set aside.

3. Heat a large skillet over medium-high heat, and add 2 tablespoons oil. Toss noodles a bit to loosen them, then place in an even layer in skillet. Cook until noodle cake browns lightly on underside, 3 to 4 minutes, then turn with a spatula and cook other side. When noodle cake is browned on both sides and heated through, transfer to a serving plate and place in a low oven to warm.

4. Heat wok over medium-high heat, and add remaining oil. Add ginger, green onion, and red-pepper flakes (if used); cook until fragrant. Add shellfish, staggering cooking times if using several types. Cook until just done (shrimp take 2 to 4 minutes, scallops 1 to 3 minutes, squid 1 minute or less). Remove from pan and set aside.

5. Add mushrooms and bok choy to wok; stir-fry until heated through. Add stock mixture, return shellfish, and cook until sauce thickens slightly. Serve over noodle cake.

Serves 4 with other dishes.

GINGER BEEF CHOW FUN

When stir-fried, fresh rice noodles are known as chow fun.

> ¼ cup minced ginger
> ½ teaspoon kosher salt
> 2 tablespoons Shaoxing wine or dry sherry
> ¼ pound boneless tender beef, thinly sliced
> ½ pound fresh, wide rice noodles
>   Oil, for stir-frying
> 2 tablespoons dark soy sauce
> ⅓ cup green onion tops, in 1½-inch pieces

1. In a small bowl, combine ginger, salt, and wine. Add beef and marinate for 30 minutes to 4 hours, turning meat occasionally in marinade.

2. Place noodles in a colander and pour boiling water over them to wash off excess oil and soften noodles slightly. Drain thoroughly.

3. Drain beef. Combine remaining marinade with soy sauce. Heat wok over medium-high heat, and add oil, beef, and green onions. Stir-fry until meat loses its raw color. Add soy sauce mixture, and toss to coat meat lightly. Remove mixture from pan.

4. Return pan to heat and add a little more oil. Add noodles and stir-fry until heated through and browned in spots. Return beef mixture to pan, toss to combine with noodles, and transfer to serving plate.

Serves 4 with other dishes.

COLD NOODLES WITH ASSORTED TOPPINGS

Cold noodles tossed with a soy sauce-sesame oil dressing are perfect for warm-weather meals. Try them plain or with cold meats and vegetables, such as those suggested below, scattered on top.

> 1 pound thin Chinese-style egg noodles, boiled and drained
> 2 tablespoons peanut oil

Basic Cold Noodle Dressing

> 3 tablespoons each *black soy sauce and sesame oil*
> 4 teaspoons *black vinegar*
> 1 tablespoon *sugar*
> ½ to 1½ teaspoons *chile oil*
> 1 teaspoon *finely minced ginger*

Suggested Toppings

> *Smithfield ham, soaked in water, drained, and thinly sliced*
> *Cantonese Roast Pork I or II (see page 87), sliced*
> *Leftover chicken, either Red-Cooked Chicken (see page 77) or White-Cooked Chicken (see page 67), shredded*
> *Small shrimp, steamed in shell and peeled*
> *Carrots, grated*
> *Cucumber, sliced as thin as possible*
> *Green onions, sliced*
> *Snow peas or green beans, blanched and sliced*
> *Bean sprouts*
> *Fresh coriander leaves*
> *Celery, sliced diagonally*
> *Peanuts or cashews, toasted and chopped*
> *Sesame seed, toasted*

1. Toss noodles with peanut oil.

2. In a large bowl, prepare Basic Cold Noodle Dressing. Add noodles and toss to coat evenly with dressing. Set aside at room temperature or in refrigerator until ready to serve, preferably overnight.

3. Prepare toppings. Vegetables may be soaked briefly in a thin mixture of rice vinegar and water or tossed in additional dressing, if desired. Toss noodles to distribute dressing, and serve in individual bowls. Arrange toppings on a serving platter and let each person add them to noodles to taste.

Serves 4 to 6 with other dishes.

Basic Cold Noodle Dressing

Combine all ingredients in a bowl large enough to hold noodles; stir to dissolve sugar.

Makes enough for 1 pound noodles.

Grated carrots, blanched snow peas, cooked shrimp, sliced cucumbers, and cashews are just a few of the possible toppings for cold, soy-dressed noodles.

SOUP NOODLES WITH SHRIMP

This dish is just one example of a whole genre: noodles in a deep bowl of broth topped with meats, seafood, or vegetables. The possibilities for toppings are endless: sliced barbecued pork, leftover roasted or smoked poultry, squid, or fish balls, to name just a few, with any number of vegetables. Recipes for soups, braised dishes, and even stir-fried dishes should suggest other toppings. To eat soup noodles in true Chinese fashion, use chopsticks in one hand and a soup spoon in the other.

- ½ pound thin Chinese-style egg noodles, boiled, rinsed, and oiled
- 4 cups Rich Chicken Stock (see page 64), salted to taste
- 1 teaspoon finely grated ginger
- 2 green onions, cut into 1-inch lengths
- ¼ pound small or medium shrimp, peeled, split lengthwise, and deveined
- 1 cup fresh or frozen peas or snow peas

Place prepared noodles in individual bowls. In a saucepan heat stock to a simmer with ginger shreds. Add green onions, shrimp, and peas; simmer until shrimp is done. Pour stock over noodles, and arrange shrimp and vegetables on top.

Serves 4.

SPICY BEAN SAUCE NOODLES
Zha jiang mein
Northern and Western China

This thick, spicy sauce can be served on hot or cold noodles. Use it sparingly, however, as it is both rich and highly seasoned. This is one place where a thicker noodle is in order, either "chow mein noodles" or Italian-style spaghetti.

- ¼ cup brown bean sauce *Chinese chile sauce with beans, to taste (see Note)*
- 3 tablespoons oil
- ⅓ pound minced pork
- 1 tablespoon each *chopped ginger and garlic*
- 2 tablespoons thinly sliced green onion
- ½ pound chow mein noodles
- 1 teaspoon sesame oil
- ¼ cup blanched, shredded snow peas, for garnish

1. Have ready a large pot of boiling salted water in which to cook the noodles. Combine bean sauce with chile sauce to taste; the mixture will be quite salty and should have quite a strong chile punch.

2. Heat wok or skillet over medium-high heat, and add 2 tablespoons oil. Add pork and stir-fry until it loses its raw color. Add ginger and garlic; cook 1 minute more, then stir in bean sauce mixture and green onion. Cook until heated through, and set aside to keep warm.

3. Boil noodles just until tender. Drain and toss with sesame oil mixed with remaining vegetable oil. Transfer to individual bowls and top with a little sauce. Garnish with snow peas.

Serves 4 to 6.

<u>Note</u> Chinese chile sauces vary widely in intensity. A teaspoon or two of one brand might give a gently hot flavor, while a half-teaspoon of another brings tears to your eyes. Adjust according to taste and according to the brand you have.

SICHUAN SPICY NOODLES IN BROTH
Don don mein
Southwestern China

Chile-flavored noodles are a favorite street food in southwestern China. Some versions are served with thick peanut or sesame sauces, others in a thin and soupy sauce like this one. Don't serve this dish on a good tablecloth, or for that matter in your best clothes, as you will undoubtedly splatter some of the chile-stained broth. Chinese chile sauce can be quite spicy. See the note of caution in the recipe for Spicy Bean Sauce Noodles (at left).

- 1 cup oil
- ¼ cup raw peanuts
- 1 tablespoon each *minced garlic and green onion Chinese chile sauce to taste*
- 2 cups Basic Chicken Stock (see page 64), lightly salted
- ½ pound thin Chinese-style egg noodles, boiled and drained *Sliced green-onion tops, for garnish*

1. Heat oil in a wok over medium heat. Fry peanuts until lightly browned and remove with a wire skimmer or slotted spoon. Drain on paper towels, allow to cool, and chop roughly. Remove all but 2 tablespoons oil from wok and reserve for another use.

2. Allow wok to cool, then return to low heat. Add garlic and green onion and cook, stirring, until quite fragrant but not browned; adjust heat so they just sizzle. Add chile sauce and cook until oil is stained red.

3. Add stock to pan and bring to a boil. Taste and adjust seasoning as necessary. Ladle sauce over noodles in individual bowls and garnish with chopped peanuts and sliced green-onion tops.

Serves 4.

BREADS AND PANCAKES

Although ovens are fairly new in Chinese cooking, breads have an ancient place in the Chinese diet. The earliest form of bread, a noodle-like dough of flour and water cooked on a flat, heated stone, is still represented today by the various flatbreads of northern China. The "Mandarin pancake" and the savory green-onion breads of Shandong are modern adaptations of this ancient technique. Both are actually quite similar to two other similarly-old foods, the Middle Eastern pita bread and the Mexican tortilla. In fact, if necessary, purchased flour tortillas can be substituted for the pancakes in Mu Shu Pork (see page 45).

Steamed breads, on the other hand, are a uniquely Chinese invention. Plain steamed rolls are a typical staple in much of the north, used to sop up sauces and soups. The plain dough can also be formed into fancy shapes such as Flower Rolls (see page 113) or stuffed with various savory or sweet ingredients to make the popular Cantonese steamed buns or *bao* (see page 113). For a discussion of steaming equipment and technique please see page 78.

To keep breads from sticking to the steamer basket or tray, the Chinese place them on squares of paper. Commercial bakeries use a silicone-treated parchment, which may be available in well-stocked cookware stores. Untreated kitchen parchment or waxed paper will probably have to be greased with shortening or oil on the side that goes against the bread.

Steamed breads can be refrigerated or frozen after steaming, and then reheated in a steamer as before. Refrigerated, they will keep for a day or two; freeze for longer storage. Thaw before steaming.

BASIC STEAMED BREAD DOUGH

This is the basic northern Chinese bread dough, used to make plain or stuffed buns in various fancy shapes. Although it is a yeast dough, it often gets an additional leavening from baking powder, which is kneaded in just before the rolls are formed. Allow a good four to six hours to make this dough; speeding up the process by adding more yeast will produce an inferior bread. Fortunately, you can slow down the process by refrigerating the dough overnight after kneading, with excellent results. This is the ideal way to make dough for a weekend dim sum brunch. Allow two hours for the dough to return to room temperature after being refrigerated.

> 2 teaspoons sugar
> 1 cup warm (90° to 100° F) water
> 1 teaspoon (half a package) active dry yeast
> 3 cups flour, plus flour for kneading
> Peanut oil and sesame oil

1. Warm a 2-quart or larger bowl with hot water; drain and wipe dry. Dissolve sugar in warm water in bowl, and sprinkle yeast over surface. Let stand 5 minutes or until mixture smells yeasty and begins to bubble on the surface.

2. Stir in 3 cups flour and mix until dough comes together in stiff clumps. Turn out onto a lightly floured board and knead until smooth and springy, 5 to 10 minutes. Add additional flour only if necessary to keep dough from sticking to board.

3. Rinse bowl with warm water, dry, and oil lightly with peanut oil and a few drops of sesame oil. Form dough into a ball, turn in bowl to oil all sides lightly, and cover with plastic wrap. Let rise in a warm place (70° to 75° F) until doubled in bulk,

45 minutes to 1 hour. Punch down, let rise again until doubled, and punch down again. Dough is now ready to be formed into buns or rolls.

Makes enough dough for 16 filled buns, 20 plain buns, 24 Flower Rolls, or 3 green-onion breads.

PLAIN STEAMED BUNS
Man tou
Northern China

Visitors to modern dining halls in northern Chinese cities describe patrons helping themselves from huge mounds of these rolls. White, bland, and vaguely sweet, they play the same role in the north as rice does in the south—they are both a filling staff of life and an absorber and cushion for stronger flavors.

> Basic Steamed Bread Dough (at left)
> Shortening or oil, for baking papers
> 1 teaspoon baking powder

1. Prepare dough as directed. Cut out twenty 2-inch squares of baking parchment or waxed paper. If using waxed paper, grease one side lightly with shortening. Set aside.

2. Sprinkle baking powder on board, and knead into dough until thoroughly incorporated. Divide dough into 20 pieces. Roll each gently into a smooth ball and set on a square of paper (greased side of paper toward dough if using waxed paper). Place rolls on a baking sheet (allow room for rising), and cover with a towel. Let rise until doubled in bulk. Steam in a bamboo steamer with a lattice cover 15 minutes, turn off heat, and let stand, covered, 5 minutes longer. Serve immediately.

Makes 20 small rolls.

Flower Rolls, tender spirals of steamed bread dough, are an ideal foil for rich duck dishes, such as this Crisp-Skin Roast Duck (see page 88).

FLOWER ROLLS

These fancy rolls, with their petals of dough separated by a layer of sesame oil, are a traditional accompaniment to roast or smoked duck.

> *Basic Steamed Bread Dough (see page 111)*
> 1 *teaspoon baking powder*
> *Shortening or oil, for baking papers*
> *Flour, for dusting*
> 2 *teaspoons sesame oil or a blend of sesame and peanut oils*

1. Prepare dough as directed. Sprinkle baking powder on board and knead into dough until thoroughly incorporated. Divide dough in half and set 1 piece aside, covered with a towel.

2. Cut out twenty-four 2-inch squares of baking parchment or waxed paper (twelve if making double flower rolls). If using waxed paper, grease 1 side lightly with shortening. Set aside.

3. Dust board with flour and roll out half the dough into a 10- by 12-inch rectangle. Rub top surface all over with 1 teaspoon sesame oil. Roll from long edge like a jelly roll. Slice roll into 12 equal pieces. Repeat with other half of dough.

4. *To make single flower rolls:* Lay a chopstick on top of a piece of dough parallel to the cut ends. Press down to reduce center to about half its thickness. Lift pinched ends, bring them together underneath the roll, and pinch together. Place roll pinched side down on a square of paper on a baking sheet, allowing room for rolls to rise. *To make double flower rolls:* Place one piece of dough on top of another and crease and fold in the same way.

5. Let rise until doubled in bulk. Steam in a bamboo steamer with a lattice cover 15 minutes. Serve immediately, or allow to cool, wrap tightly, and freeze for future use.

Makes 2 dozen single or 1 dozen double rolls.

STEAMED PORK BUNS
Char siu bao
Southern China

Bao, or stuffed steamed buns, are among the most popular dim sum items. This version with barbecued pork is the most common, but there are also versions with other meats or sweetened pastes of beans or seeds.

> *Basic Steamed Bread Dough (see page 111)*
> 1 *tablespoon oil*
> 2 *teaspoons each minced ginger and garlic*
> ¼ *cup sliced green onion*
> ½ *pound Cantonese-style barbecued pork, in ¼-inch cubes (see Note)*
> 1 *teaspoon red bean curd (optional)*
> 1 *teaspoon cornstarch dissolved in ¼ cup water or stock*
> 2 *tablespoons soy sauce*
> *Shortening or oil, for baking papers*
> 1 *teaspoon baking powder*
> *Flour, for dusting*

1. Prepare dough as directed. Prepare filling while dough is rising for the second time.

2. *To prepare filling:* Heat wok or skillet over medium heat, and add oil. Add ginger, garlic, and green onion; stir-fry until fragrant. Add pork, red bean curd (if used), cornstarch mixture, and soy sauce; cook until thickened. Taste for seasoning and adjust if necessary. Allow to cool.

3. Cut out sixteen 2½-inch squares of baking parchment or waxed paper. If using waxed paper, grease 1 side lightly with shortening. Set aside.

4. Punch dough down. Sprinkle baking powder on board and knead into dough until thoroughly incorporated. Divide dough into 16 even pieces and cover with a towel. Lightly flour board and roll a piece of dough out into a 4-inch circle. With rolling pin at edge of dough, roll inward to within 1 inch of center. Give dough a quarter turn and repeat. Continue rolling edge thinner until circle reaches a diameter of 5 to 6 inches; center will be twice as thick as edges.

5. Place 1½ tablespoons of filling in center of dough. Lift one edge of dough and pinch a pleat between thumb and forefinger. Keeping thumb in place, gather remaining dough in a series of pleats in the same direction, working around the circle. Finish with a twist to seal. Place bun pleated side down on a square of paper. Repeat with remaining dough and filling.

6. Place buns on a baking sheet (allow room for rising). Let rise until nearly doubled in bulk, 30 minutes to 1 hour. Steam in a bamboo steamer with a lattice cover 15 minutes, turn off heat, and let rest 5 minutes. Serve immediately. Leftover steamed buns may be refrigerated for a few days or frozen for longer storage. Freeze buns unwrapped on a baking sheet. When frozen, transfer to a tightly sealed plastic bag. Reheat in a steamer 10 to 15 minutes.

Makes 16 buns (4 to 8 servings).

Note Cantonese-style "barbecued" pork is available in Chinese delis, or you can make it yourself; see Cantonese Roast Pork I and II, page 87.

Variation Slice 3 or 4 Chinese sausages (*lop cheong*) in half lengthwise, then diagonally into ¼-inch slices. Steam in a bowl 10 minutes and discard rendered fat. Use sausage in place of roast pork and omit red bean curd.

Variation Boil ½ cup dried lotus seed (available in Chinese groceries) in 1 cup water until tender. Grind to a paste in a food processor with 1½ teaspoons minced candied ginger, 1 teaspoon sugar, 2 tablespoons water, and ¼ teaspoon salt. Use as filling.

Variation Any of the varieties of bao can also be baked. Brush tops with a sweetened egg wash and bake at 350° F until golden brown, 20 to 25 minutes.

NORTHERN CHINA

We tend to think of rice as the staple food of all of China. Yet the entire northern half of the country, which includes the fertile Yellow River plain as well as the sparsely populated regions to the northeast and northwest, is either too cold or too dry to grow rice. This is China's wheat country. Breads and noodles are the staple foods here, along with vegetables more suited to the cooler climate.

Beijing (Peking), the capital, is the home of the cuisine known in restaurants in the United States as "Mandarin." The name is actually that of the Beijing dialect, the official national language of China. The word *mandarin* originally meant an official of the imperial court, and has come to refer to all aspects of court culture. The court attracted cooks and foodstuffs from throughout China.

Northern cuisines reflect the food resources of the area. In addition to wheat, millet, and other grains, soybeans are a major crop, and tofu is an important source of protein. Hoisin sauce and other soybean sauces and condiments are typical ingredients. Cabbages, green onions, leeks, and garlic are widely used here, where the growing season is shorter than in the south.

Beijing food also shows a strong influence of centuries of trade along the Silk Route, which wound across northwest China to Afghanistan and eventually to the Middle East. There is a strong Moslem influence on the cuisine of the region, most notably a preference for lamb and mutton over pork. Grilling at the table and "hot-pot" cooking are also characteristic of this nomadic culture.

Other northern specialties include the steamed rolls and green-onion cakes of Shandong, the sweet-and-sour carp of Henan, and the fried dumplings known as potstickers. Swallow's nests from the cliffs of Shandong province are used all over China to make bird's nest soup.

MANDARIN PANCAKES

Try these thin, soft breads with duck or mu shu dishes.

> 2 cups flour
> ¾ cup boiling water
> 2 tablespoons peanut oil
> 1 teaspoon sesame oil

1. Place flour in a bowl and add water gradually, stirring with a fork or chopsticks until dough comes together in clumps. Turn dough out onto a lightly floured board and knead until dough springs back when pressed with a finger, about 5 minutes. Dough should be slightly moister and denser than a bread dough, but not sticky. Cover with plastic wrap and set aside to rest 30 minutes.

2. Roll dough into a 2-inch-diameter log. With a knife or dough cutter, cut in half. Slice each half in half again, then divide each quarter into 4 even slices (or 3 for larger pancakes). Cover with a towel to prevent drying.

3. Heat a heavy skillet over medium-low heat. Oil surface lightly with 1 tablespoon peanut oil, and wipe away excess with a folded paper towel (save towel for reapplying oil if necessary later on). Combine remaining peanut oil with sesame oil and set aside.

4. Flatten a piece of dough with the heel of your hand and roll into a 3-inch circle. Repeat with another ball. Brush the tops lightly with oil mixture and lay one on top of the other, oiled sides together. Roll out to a diameter of 6 inches (see Note). Place double pancake in skillet and cook until lightly blistered but not browned, about 45 seconds per side. Meanwhile, roll out next pair of pancakes.

5. Remove cooked pancakes to a plate or basket lined with a towel. Fold towel over pancakes to keep warm. Continue rolling and cooking pancakes with rest of dough. Adjust heat if necessary to keep pancakes from browning too fast. After they have cooled for a minute or so, peel halves apart. (Pancakes may be prepared up to this point several hours ahead of use.)

6. Steam for 10 minutes before serving.

Makes 16 small (6-inch) or 12 large (8-inch) pancakes.

Note For a neater appearance, roll pancakes 1 inch larger than the desired size. Using a small bowl as a guide, cut around the rim to remove the thick edges of the pancakes.

GREEN-ONION CAKES
Northern China

These thick flatbreads, enriched with oil and fragrant with minced green onion, are a specialty of Shandong province. They can be made with a raised dough, or as follows, with an unleavened dough.

> Dough for Mandarin Pancakes (at left)
> Flour, for dusting
> 2 to 3 teaspoons sesame oil
> Kosher salt
> ½ cup finely minced green onion
> Oil, for preparing pan

1. Prepare dough through kneading and resting stage (step 1). Divide dough in half. Roll 1 piece out on a floured surface to an oblong shape 12 to 14 inches long. Rub a generous teaspoon of sesame oil over the surface of the dough to within 1 inch of the edges. Sprinkle evenly with salt, and scatter half the green onion over the surface, again stopping 1 inch from the edge.

2. Roll up dough into a long cylinder. Coil the rolled dough into a spiral shape and tuck end underneath edge. Roll out coil to a 10-inch circle. Repeat with other piece of dough. (Dough may be prepared to this point and refrigerated or frozen.)

3. Heat a griddle or heavy skillet over medium-low heat. Oil pan generously and cook cakes, one at a time, until covered with brown blisters, about 5 minutes per side. Serve hot, cut into wedges.

Makes 2 large cakes, 2 to 4 servings.

DIM SUM

Every region of China has its special snack foods, many of them small tidbits wrapped in noodlelike skins or bread dough and then steamed or fried. This kind of snacking has been taken to the greatest heights in the south, particularly in the teahouses of Guangzhou (Canton). Here, and in Cantonese-style teahouses in every overseas Chinese community, these morsels are known as dim sum. The name is variously translated as "little hearts," "dot hearts," or "to touch the heart." However you translate it, dim sum is a delightful invention and can serve as anything from a light snack to a full meal.

In a typical teahouse, dim sum is served from midmorning to mid- or late afternoon. There is no menu; instead, a group of servers wheel carts around the dining room, calling out the names of the item or two they are carrying. Stacks of steamer baskets may hold steamed dumplings, puffy steamed breads, simmered duck's feet, braised spareribs, or sheets of fresh rice noodles wrapped around bits of meat and vegetables. Some carts have built-in woks in which the servers whip up noodle dishes or soups at tableside. Customers indicate which items they would like (pointing if they don't speak Cantonese), and when it comes time to total up the bill, the waiters simply count the plates on the table and charge by the number of plates.

Of course, you don't need to offer all the variety of a Hong Kong teahouse to serve a selection of dim sum. The following recipes include some dim sum favorites, which can be used either alone as appetizers or for a weekend dim sum brunch (see "Dim Sum Brunch," page 121).

WRAPPERS

Ground meat or seafood stuffings wrapped in small rounds or squares of noodlelike dough are among the most popular dim sum items. Wrappers for these dumplings and rolls come in a wide range of sizes and shapes, which can be a little bewildering.

Even more than shape, thickness is the key to the suitability of a given wrapper for a given type of dumpling. Chinese noodle manufacturers make round wrappers of three different thicknesses in nearly identical packages. The thinnest of these (48 per inch), used for the delicate steamed dumplings called *siu mai,* are labeled *su my* (or some similar spelling) skins. Slightly thicker (32 per inch) are *sue gow* skins, meant for boiled dumplings. Thickest of all, at 16 per inch, are potsticker skins or *kuo teh* wrappers. The different thicknesses are not interchangeable; potsticker skins would make a terribly tough wrapping for steamed dumplings, and potstickers made with thin siu mai skins would undoubtedly fall apart during cooking.

Square wrappers come in two basic sizes—3½ inches square for wontons and 7 to 8 inches square for spring rolls. Wonton skins vary in thickness, but spring-roll skins should be as thin as possible. Spring rolls can also be made with a thin, eggless batter cooked in a pan like a crêpe (Philippine *lumpia* wrappers are a near equivalent) or even in sheets of bean-curd skin soaked until pliable.

Japanese-style noodle manufacturers make wrappers similar to the Chinese types. One widely available brand includes "*gyoza*—round wonton wraps," 32 wrappers per inch thickness of dough, and square wonton wraps at 36 wrappers per inch thickness of dough. They also make spring-roll skins that are a little smaller than the Chinese type at 6 inches square.

Storebought wrappers will keep for a week or two if tightly wrapped in the refrigerator, or longer if frozen. For best results, remove from the original package and rewrap with plastic wrap.

Homemade Wrappers

If fresh wrappers are not available, it's easy to make your own from fresh noodle dough. The thinnest setting on a typical pasta machine is a little thick for *siu mai* and spring rolls, so roll the sheets a little thinner with a rolling pin, or stretch them by hand to the desired thickness before cutting out rounds with a 3½-inch cutter. For potstickers, use the next-to-thinnest setting. By the way, there is no need to buy a special cutter; an empty can from bamboo shoots or water chestnuts is just the right size.

Most dumplings can be made ahead of time and frozen. Place unwrapped on a baking sheet and freeze; as soon as they solidify, transfer to a plastic bag or container and seal tightly. Cook directly from freezer, allowing a few minutes extra cooking time. Keep one or two varieties on hand for an instant appetizer.

STUFFINGS

Although the dim sum recipes in this chapter specify stuffings, in most cases the stuffings can be used interchangeably. An exception is the translucent shrimp dumpling called *har gow*, which just doesn't seem right made with anything but a seafood filling. Here are three basic stuffing recipes and a few variations.

PORK AND CABBAGE STUFFING

Ground pork is the basic ingredient of most Chinese stuffings for dumplings, pastries, and vegetables. The cabbage adds mostly bulk, plus a little texture.

- *½ cup shredded cabbage (bok choy, Napa, or any green variety)*
- *½ teaspoon salt*
- *1 pound boneless pork*
- *¼ cup each minced green onion and minced bamboo shoots*
- *1 tablespoon minced ginger*
- *2 tablespoons each soy sauce and Shaoxing wine or dry sherry*
- *1 teaspoon sesame oil*
- *1 egg*
- *1 teaspoon cornstarch*

Toss cabbage with salt and place in a colander to drain 30 minutes. Squeeze out excess moisture. Grind pork finely in a food processor, or mince by hand to a fine texture. In a large bowl, combine pork, drained and squeezed cabbage, green onions, bamboo shoots, ginger, soy sauce, wine, oil, egg, and cornstarch; blend thoroughly.

Makes 2 cups.

Variation Substitute beef, lamb, or dark meat from chicken or turkey for the pork in the variation above.

Pork and Mushroom Stuffing

Add ¼ cup soaked and minced black mushrooms (about 3 caps) to Pork and Cabbage Stuffing.

PORK AND SHRIMP STUFFING

A coarse texture is ideal for larger dumplings and spring rolls; for smaller dumplings such as Cantonese Pork Dumplings or Wontons or for stuffing steamed vegetables, mince the carrots and chop the shrimp a little more finely.

- *½ pound boneless pork*
- *½ pound shrimp, peeled and roughly chopped*
- *¼ cup each minced green onion and minced water chestnuts*
- *4 teaspoons minced ginger*
- *¼ cup finely shredded carrot*
- *2 tablespoons each soy sauce and Shaoxing wine or sherry*
- *1 teaspoon sesame oil*
- *1 egg*

Grind pork finely in a food processor, or mince by hand to a fine texture. Combine with shrimp, green onion, water chestnuts, ginger, carrot, soy sauce, wine, sesame oil, and egg.

Makes 2 cups.

VEGETARIAN STUFFING

Here is a vegetarian alternative for stuffing dumplings and wontons. The combination of fresh and fried tofu and egg white gives it a light but meaty texture. Nonvegetarians will like it, too!

- *1 clove garlic*
  ¾-inch slice ginger, peeled
- *¼ cup cashews, toasted*
- *½ package (3½ oz) fried tofu*
- *½ package (3½ oz) fresh tofu, drained*
- *2 teaspoons each soy sauce and Shaoxing wine or sherry*
- *1 teaspoon sesame oil*
- *1 egg white*
- *2 tablespoons each minced green onion and finely diced carrot*
- *2 dried black mushroom caps, soaked and finely diced*
- *2 tablespoons chopped coriander leaves (optional)*

To prepare with a food processor: Close cover and turn machine on. Add garlic, ginger, and cashews through feed tube and process to a fine grind. Break fried tofu into small pieces and crumble fresh tofu; add both through feed tube along with soy sauce, wine, and sesame oil; process to a paste. Transfer mixture to a medium-sized bowl and blend in egg white, green onion, carrot, mushroom, and coriander (if used). *To prepare by hand:* Mince garlic, ginger, and cashews together as finely as possible. Mince fried tofu. In a bowl, mash fresh tofu to a paste and blend in soy sauce, wine, sesame oil, egg white, green onion, carrot, mushrooms, and coriander. Beat with a spoon to a smooth consistency.

Makes 1¼ cups.

POTSTICKERS
Northern China

These northern-style dumplings have become popular in southern China as well as overseas. They get their name from their method of cooking, a combination of pan-frying and steaming that causes the bottoms to stick to the pan slightly. Getting just the right amount of "stick" without destroying the dumplings takes a little practice, so don't despair if the first few batches tear when you try to lift them from the pan. Practice cooking this dish with family or not-too-fussy friends.

- *2 cups of one of the following stuffings:*
  Pork and Cabbage Stuffing (at left)
  Pork and Mushroom Stuffing (at left)
  Vegetarian Stuffing (at left)
- *½ pound potsticker skins or 1 recipe Chinese Egg Noodle Dough (see page 107)*
  Oil, for frying
- *¾ cup water or thinned Basic Chicken Stock (see page 64)*
  Soy sauce, chile oil, and black or rice vinegar, for dipping, or one or more dipping sauces (see page 36)

1. Prepare stuffing as directed. If making your own skins, prepare noodle dough as directed and roll out to a thickness of $1/16$ inch, then cut into $3\frac{1}{2}$-inch circles.

2. Place 1 heaping teaspoonful across center of a skin and lightly moisten entire edge with a little water. Lift both sides of skin and pinch together in center of arc, above stuffing. Working on one side of center at a time, pleat near edge of skin toward center and pinch against far edge to seal. Continue working outward making 3 or 4 pleats in all. Repeat on other side of center. Dumpling will naturally curl away from pleats to form a flat-bottomed crescent with a pleated ridge across top.

3. Heat a heavy, flat-bottomed skillet (nonstick or well-seasoned cast iron) with a tight-fitting lid over medium-high heat. Add enough oil to generously coat bottom. Arrange dumplings in pan in a closely packed circle, pleated sides up. Cook until edges begin to show browning on bottom. Add the water or stock (careful—it will splatter a bit), and immediately cover pan. Reduce heat to medium and cook until dumplings have swollen and liquid is nearly evaporated, 6 to 8 minutes.

4. Remove lid and increase heat to medium-high. Cook until liquid boils away and dumplings begin to sizzle in remaining oil. If oil is nearly all gone, add a little more for the final browning. Continue cooking until bottoms become crisp and golden brown. Loosen with a spatula and transfer to serving plate. Set table with individual bowls for each diner to use for a dipping sauce.

Makes 16 potstickers, 4 to 8 servings.

Two different cooking techniques—pan-frying and steaming—give Potstickers their unique combination of crisp, browned bottoms and tender tops. Try them with an assortment of meat-based or vegetarian stuffings.

117

TEA TIME, CHINESE STYLE

Tea is the most popular beverage in China, but not necessarily at mealtime. For centuries, the Chinese have enjoyed a cup of tea as a delicious and refreshing beverage, a mild stimulant, and an aid to digestion.

Because a pot of tea typically lands on the table of a Chinese restaurant along with the menus, many people assume that tea is always drunk with Chinese meals. While this is true in some tea-growing regions, in much of China tea is served only after or between meals.

Chinese teas are available in most Asian groceries, usually in brightly decorated packages. Shopping for Chinese tea can be an endless fascination, especially if you are willing to try new types. Look for a store that carries a large variety of teas, and one that is busy enough that it turns over its stock frequently. Don't take the names too literally. Dragon Well, a famous green tea from near Hangzhou, is a widely used name for any tea of the same general type.

TEA TYPES

There are countless varieties of Chinese tea, differing in color and flavor according to where they are grown and how they are processed. But they can be grouped into four main categories: fermented (black or "red"), unfermented (green), semifermented (oolong), and flavored teas. (Theoretically, any tea could be produced in green, black, or semifermented form, but local traditions generally dictate which method is used.)

Black tea is the type most familiar to Westerners. It makes a deep reddish-brown brew, full of flavor but not as strong as the black teas of India and Sri Lanka (formerly Ceylon). The tea leaves are allowed to ferment before drying, giving them a longer shelf life. This is strictly a between-meals beverage, as it is too strong to go with most foods. *Pu-Erh* from Yunnan province and *Keemun* from Anhui province are among China's best-known black teas.

Green tea is the opposite of black—pale in color, delicate in flavor and aroma. Leaves for green tea are steamed immediately after harvesting to prevent fermentation. This is the type of tea most favored by the Japanese, and it tastes better when served with food than do the stronger black teas. Dragon Well and Gunpowder are two well-known Chinese green teas.

Oolong, or semifermented, teas are given an intermediate treatment—they are allowed to ferment partially and then steamed to stop the process. As would be expected, they are intermediate in flavor and body between green and black teas, and they go especially well with foods. A specialty of the eastern provinces and Taiwan, this category actually covers a whole spectrum between green and black teas. One particularly famous oolong is *Ti Kuan Yin* (*Tit Koon Yum* in Cantonese), "Iron Goddess of Mercy," originally from Fujian province and also grown on Taiwan. It is typically brewed quite strong and served in tiny cups.

Flavored teas include green teas and oolongs flavored with other ingredients, such as chrysanthemum or jasmine blossoms or litchi fruit, and the smoked black Lapsang Souchong. Chrysanthemum tea goes especially well with dim sum, whereas sweeter-scented teas are better by themselves.

All tea should be stored in a tightly sealed container in a cool place. Even in its container, tea loses some of its flavor and aroma with time, so try to buy it in small quantities and use it up fairly soon after opening. Most Chinese tea is sold in bulk, which lasts longer than tea bags.

There are different views on the proper temperature of brewing water. Some experts call for rapidly boiling water for all teas; others say that water that has not quite reached the boil is better for the more delicate green teas and oolongs. Hotter water will extract more flavor, which may or may not be an advantage.

ALMOND COOKIES

These cookies are a Chinese-American invention, and a very popular one. A good almond cookie is thick and slightly rounded on top, with a cracked surface over a tender, crumbly center. The key to this texture is to cream the shortening and sugar together thoroughly, incorporating plenty of tiny air bubbles. Allow a good two to three minutes in an electric mixer, longer with a hand-held mixer or if beating by hand.

- ¾ cup butter, shortening, lard, or a combination
- 1 cup sugar
- 1 egg
- 1 teaspoon almond extract
- ½ cup ground almonds
- 2 cups flour
- 1½ teaspoons baking powder
- ⅛ teaspoon table salt (omit if using salted butter)
- 1 egg white mixed with 1 tablespoon water
- 36 whole blanched almonds (optional)

1. Preheat oven to 375° F. In a large bowl, using a tabletop mixer with a paddle-shaped beater or a hand-held mixer, cream butter and sugar to a very light, fluffy consistency. Add whole egg, almond extract, and ground almonds; blend thoroughly.

2. In a small bowl, sift together flour, baking powder, and salt. Add to sugar mixture and blend thoroughly. Do not overwork dough. (The dough can be prepared ahead of time and refrigerated.)

3. Pinch off tablespoonfuls of dough and roll into 1¼-inch balls. Place balls 2 inches apart on greased cookie sheets. Flatten balls slightly with the heel of the hand. Brush lightly with egg white mixture. Press an almond into the top of each cookie, if desired. Bake in lower third of oven until bottoms are lightly browned and edges just begin to show browning, but tops are still pale, 12 to 15 minutes. Remove cookies from pan to cool on wire racks.

Makes 3 dozen small (2¼-inch) cookies.

HOW TO MAKE THE PERFECT POT OF TEA

1. Heat the pot. Tea should be brewed only in ceramic or glass pots or cups, never in metal, which might impart a metallic taste. A good teapot should hold enough water for several cups, but not so much that the tea gets cold or too strong before the pot is finished. A pot with small holes at the base of the spout will strain out the leaves when the tea is poured, making further straining unnecessary; if a few leaves wind up in the cup, they will sink harmlessly to the bottom. If you prefer to brew tea directly in the cup, look for a traditional large Chinese teacup with a lid; the lid keeps the water hot while the tea brews, and the leaves sink to the bottom.

2. Add tea. Allow a teaspoonful of tea leaves per person served (not per cup, as is often recommended). If your pot has a built-in strainer, add the tea leaves loose.

3. Add hot water. Classical Chinese texts on tea specify at great length what kind of water to use, and there is no doubt that tea tastes especially good made with water fresh from a mountain spring. However, unless you have a spring handy, any good-tasting water will do. If your tap water is not very tasty, you might want to use bottled water for brewing tea.

4. Brew the tea. Brewing time is a matter of personal taste, but anywhere from 3 to 5 minutes is usually sufficient to make a light, refreshing cup. Of course, if you prefer a stronger cup, allow a longer brewing time. Milk, sugar, and lemon have nothing to offer to most Chinese teas; if you prefer tea that way, stick to the strongest black Keemun types or Indian tea.

Most Chinese teas can take a second and even a third extraction. In fact, the second extraction often has a cleaner, less bitter flavor than the first. Some connoisseurs routinely discard the first water after a minute or two of brewing, and then refill the pot and brew as usual.

*Are wontons Chinese ravi-
oli, or are ravioli Italian
wontons? The argument
over which came first may
never be settled, but the
wonton—steamed, fried,
or simmered in soup—is
one of the world's favorite
stuffed pasta creations.*

WONTONS

Probably the most familiar Chinese
dumpling to Westerners is the wonton, a relatively large skin wrapped
around a small amount of stuffing.
While they are most often served in
soup, they can also be fried or
steamed. Fried, they go well with
tangy sweet and sour sauces or mustard dips; steamed, they are best with
soy sauce dips.

> *1 pound wonton skins*
> *1 pound seasoned ground pork,
>   or 2 cups of one of the
>   stuffings on page 116*
> *Oil, for deep-frying (optional)*

1. Have at hand a small bowl of
water with a brush for sealing edges.
Peel off 2 or 3 wonton skins and
place on the table, one corner
("south") toward you. Keep remaining skins covered with a towel to
prevent drying.

2. Place a scant teaspoonful of pork
or stuffing just south of center of
skin. Brush near edges lightly with
water and fold south corner over
stuffing to within ½ inch of north.
Press edges to seal. Pick up east and
west corners and bring together at
south end. Pinch or twist slightly to
seal corners together. Repeat with
remaining skins and stuffing.

3. Keep finished wontons covered
with a towel to keep them from
drying; or freeze on a baking sheet
and transfer to plastic bags when
fully frozen. Boil in plain or lightly
salted water before adding to soup,
steam 6 to 8 minutes as a simple
appetizer, or deep-fry in 375° F oil
until golden brown and crisp.

Makes 60 to 70 wontons.

DIM SUM BRUNCH

Cantonese Pork Dumplings

Steamed Shrimp Turnovers

Shanghai Spring Rolls

*Steamed Pork Buns
(see page 113)*

Ham and Cabbage Lo Mein

*Almond Cookies
(see page 119)*

*Beverage Suggestion:
Chrysanthemum or
Oolong Tea*

To the Chinese, the invitation "Yum cha" means "Let's have tea," but also "Let's have dim sum." Any day of the week, but especially on weekends, Cantonese-style teahouses from Hong Kong to London are full of Chinese families enjoying these delightful little steamed, fried, and baked morsels with a fragrant pot of tea. Entertain friends and family by turning your dining room into a Chinese teahouse for a weekend brunch.

PREPARATION PLAN

An informal weekend brunch is a perfect time to enjoy a variety of dim sum dishes. With a few friends helping out in the kitchen, it's not difficult to serve an assortment of dishes. Once again, organization is the key. Much of the preparation can be done ahead of time. With the steamed bun dough and stuffing made the night before, the Almond Cookies baked a day or two ahead, and a batch of Spring Rolls in the freezer ready to be fried, all that remains to do is the stuffing (that's what friends are for) and cooking.

To estimate the quantities needed, allow 8 to 10 pieces in all per person. This menu will feed 10 to 12 people (based on a single recipe of each item). For a larger group, either add more items or increase the recipes. If you want to make a more substantial meal, add a simple *lo mein* with boiled ham and Chinese cabbage. Other possibilities include fried chicken wings or shrimp, steamed vegetables, or rice topped with cooked meats.

Set each place with a tea cup, chopsticks, a small plate, and a small bowl for dipping sauces. A soup spoon is also handy, especially for dumplings that are to be eaten in several bites; holding the spoon under your chopsticks with the other hand (to catch falling dumplings) is perfectly acceptable, and can prevent some messy accidents.

Set a variety of condiments for each person to blend into dipping sauces. Soy sauce, vinegar (either white or black), and chile oil are the basics; other possibilities include Hot Mustard Sauce and Sweet and Sour Dipping Sauce (see page 36), and the various canned Chinese chile sauces.

Depending on the number of guests, you might serve one variety of tea or several. A good selection might include a light green tea such as Dragon Well, a medium-bodied oolong, and a flower-flavored tea such as chrysanthemum or jasmine. Strong black teas are less appropriate with dim sum. Whether you serve one tea or many, you will probably want to have several teapots brewing at once. Having a large kettle of hot water ready will make it easier to brew a steady supply of tea.

While tea is the traditional accompaniment to dim sum, you could also serve these little morsels as part of a Western-style Champagne brunch. The Chinese might find the idea shocking, but a dry or slightly sweet sparkling wine goes quite well with dim sum, as it does with most "little foods."

CANTONESE PORK DUMPLINGS
Siu mai

  24 *siu mai wrappers, packaged
        or homemade (see page 115)*
    2 *cups Pork and Cabbage or
        Pork and Mushroom Stuffing
        (see page 116)
        Soy sauce and sesame oil*

1. Place a wrapper in the palm of one hand and place 1 heaping tablespoon of stuffing in the center. Gently fold up sides of wrapper around stuffing, pressing wrapper against stuffing in 4 or 5 places. Pick up remaining folds of wrapper and press them in against stuffing, gradually shaping dumpling into an open-topped cylinder. Try to avoid large pleats in the wrapper, which will be tougher after steaming than a series of tiny folds.

2. Steam on a bamboo steamer with a lattice cover 20 to 25 minutes. Just before serving, drizzle with a little soy sauce mixed with sesame oil, if desired.

Makes 2 dozen dumplings.

STEAMED SHRIMP TURNOVERS
Har gow

These dumplings are as pretty as they are delicious. A delicate, translucent skin surrounds a pale pink filling of minced shrimp studded with bits of ginger and water chestnut and flecked with green coriander.

> 1 cup wheat starch (see Note)
> ⅓ cup cornstarch, plus cornstarch for dusting
> ¾ teaspoon kosher salt
> 1 cup boiling water
> ½ pound raw shrimp, peeled and deveined
> 1 tablespoon minced ginger
> ¼ cup minced water chestnuts
> 1 tablespoon coriander leaves, minced
> 1 egg white
> 2 teaspoons cornstarch dissolved in 1 tablespoon Shaoxing wine
> 3 tablespoons oil
> Soy sauce, vinegar, and chile oil, for dipping

1. In a medium bowl, combine wheat starch, cornstarch, and ¼ teaspoon salt. Add the boiling water and stir until well blended. Cover dough and set aside to rest 10 to 15 minutes.

2. Mince shrimp finely; combine with ginger, water chestnuts, coriander, egg white, remaining ½ teaspoon salt, and cornstarch-wine mixture. Blend thoroughly.

3. On a surface lightly dusted with cornstarch, knead dough until smooth. Rub with 1 tablespoon oil and knead until thoroughly blended. Knead in remaining oil, 1 tablespoon at a time.

4. Divide dough into quarters. Roll a piece of dough into a 1-inch-thick log and divide into 6 equal pieces. Flatten a slice of dough with the heel of the hand and roll out as thinly as possible without tearing (keep remaining dough covered with a damp towel to prevent drying). Cut a neat circle with a 3½-inch cutter and discard trimmings.

5. Place a tablespoon of filling in middle of circle of dough. Fold one side over to form a half-circle, and pinch edge to seal. Continue with remaining dough and filling, keeping dough and finished dumplings covered to prevent drying.

6. Steam dumplings on an oiled bamboo steamer with a lattice cover until skins are translucent and filling is cooked, 15 to 20 minutes. Serve with soy sauce and vinegar or chile oil for dipping.

Makes 2 dozen dumplings.

Note Wheat starch, which looks and feels like cornstarch, is sold in 1-pound bags in Chinese groceries. It contains less gluten than wheat flour. There is no substitute.

SHANGHAI SPRING ROLLS

When these are made with an egg-noodle wrapper, they are known as egg rolls. If packaged spring-roll skins are too thick, roll them through the thinnest setting of a pasta machine to yield a rectangle twice the original size, and cut them in half.

> 16 square spring-roll wrappers
> Pork and Shrimp Stuffing (see page 116)
> ¼ cup bean sprouts, cut into 2-inch lengths, or finely shredded bamboo shoots
> Oil, for deep-frying

1. Place a wrapper with one edge toward you. Spread 1 tablespoon stuffing along the near edge to within ½ inch of ends. Lay a few bean sprouts or bamboo-shoot shreds alongside stuffing. Roll up slightly to cover stuffing, fold in sides to seal ends, and roll up in remaining wrapper. Moisten edge with a little water or egg white to seal. Repeat with remaining rolls.

2. Heat oil in frying pan to 375° F. Fry rolls, a few at a time, until golden brown. Check a roll to make sure stuffing has thoroughly cooked, and adjust temperature or cooking time as necessary. Serve whole, or cut into bite-sized pieces.

Makes 16 rolls.

HAM AND CABBAGE LO MEIN

Serve this simple noodle dish if your brunch guest list is quite large. It also makes an excellent one-dish weeknight dinner.

> 2 to 3 tablespoons oil
> 1 tablespoon ginger, grated
> 2 green onions, cut into 1-inch lengths
> ½ cup shredded ham (thick shreds if using boiled ham, thinner shreds if using Smithfield)
> 2 or 3 stalks bok choy or choy sum, cut into 2-inch slices
> ½ pound fresh or dried Chinese-style egg noodles, boiled, drained, cooled, and lightly oiled
> ¼ cup Basic or Rich Chicken Stock (see page 64)
> 1 tablespoon dark soy sauce

1. Heat wok over medium-high heat, and add 1 tablespoon of the oil. Add ginger and green onion; cook until fragrant. Add ham and bok choy; stir-fry 1 minute, then transfer to a warm plate.

2. Wipe wok clean with a paper towel, and add another 1 or 2 tablespoons of oil. Reduce heat to medium. Swirl wok to cover sides with oil, then add noodles. Cook without stirring 1 minute, then begin stirring and tossing noodles to brown them in places. Add a little more oil if necessary to keep noodles from sticking.

3. When noodles are heated through and lightly browned in places, add stock and soy sauce; stir to loosen noodles from pan. Return ham and bok choy mixture to pan; toss with noodles. Increase heat to high, and continue cooking and stirring until liquid is nearly gone. Transfer to serving plate. Arrange with some ham and vegetables on top.

For a new twist on weekend entertaining, serve dim sum—an assortment of steamed, fried, and baked snacks. Brunch menu recipes begin on page 121.

INDEX

124

125

U.S. MEASURE AND METRIC MEASURE CONVERSION CHART

Formulas for Exact Measures

Rounded Measures for Quick Reference

	Symbol	When you know:	Multiply by:	To find:			
Mass (Weight)	oz	ounces	28.35	grams	1 oz		= 30 g
	lb	pounds	0.45	kilograms	4 oz		= 115 g
	g	grams	0.035	ounces	8 oz		= 225 g
	kg	kilograms	2.2	pounds	16 oz	= 1 lb	= 450 g
					32 oz	= 2 lb	= 900 g
					36 oz	= 2¼ lb	= 1,000 g (1 kg)
Volume	tsp	teaspoons	5.0	milliliters	¼ tsp	= ¹⁄₂₄ oz	= 1 ml
	tbsp	tablespoons	15.0	milliliters	½ tsp	= ¹⁄₁₂ oz	= 2 ml
	fl oz	fluid ounces	29.57	milliliters	1 tsp	= ⅙ oz	= 5 ml
	c	cups	0.24	liters	1 tbsp	= ½ oz	= 15 ml
	pt	pints	0.47	liters	1 c	= 8 oz	= 250 ml
	qt	quarts	0.95	liters	2 c (1 pt)	= 16 oz	= 500 ml
	gal	gallons	3.785	liters	4 c (1 qt)	= 32 oz	= 1 l
	ml	milliliters	0.034	fluid ounces	4 qt (1 gal)	= 128 oz	= 3¾ l
Temperature	°F	Fahrenheit	$\frac{5}{9}$ (after subtracting 32)	Celsius	32° F		= 0° C
					68° F		= 20° C
	°C	Celsius	$\frac{9}{5}$ (then add 32)	Fahrenheit	212° F		= 100° C